MW00761794

Wake Up Call One ...
It's A Wake Up Call Y'all!

Recognize What's Really Going On!

by

Ruth Isaacs

Bloomington, IN Milton Keynes, UK

authorHOUSE®

AuthorHouse™
1663 Liberty Drive, Suite 200
Bloomington, IN 47403
www.authorhouse.com
Phone: 1-800-839-8640

AuthorHouse™ UK Ltd.
500 Avebury Boulevard
Central Milton Keynes, MK9 2BE
www.authorhouse.co.uk
Phone: 08001974150

First published by AuthorHouse 8/6/2007

ISBN: 978-1-4259-4118-5 (sc)

Printed in the United States of America
Bloomington, Indiana

This book is printed on acid-free paper.

Contents

DEDICATION

To the Spirits of The Infinite Spirit
Sent to me
So that their precious Spirits
Will Recognize
That they are the children of
The Infinite Spirit
Temporarily called
My Children and Grandchildren
Darnell, Deserie, Michelle
Jennifer, Anthony, Ralph, Coron
You helped me awaken to
Strength, Courage, and the Will
To Live Life
To the Maximum
I Love You All Dearly

A special thanks to The Infinite Spirit of All That Is for the Marvelous
Energy of Being. I thank You for Your Infinite Guidance, Protection,
Wisdom, and Love. This is my devotion to You!

Get ready
The truth is coming out
Everywhere
It is like a spell has been broken
A mask has been lifted

The truth my friends
The truth is in the air
All the lies are being revealed
More and more everyday
The days of reciprocity are here

The truth my friends
Get ready for the truth
Most importantly
Know you-your Spirit and
Be of the truth

Love breathes life

Into the heart

Bringing grace

To the body

AUTHOR UNKNOWN

Feel the beauty and peace of that. Marvelous! Simply marvelous!

PREFACE

I felt the need to write this book because in many of the dimensions I explored and experienced, I felt you crying, dying and needing a way out of the programming dimensions of madness.

I write so that you will put your programming dimensions of troubles, miseries and unhappiness in their proper perspective for your Spirit. The programming is growing into sheer wickedness and is not going to get any better unless the prevailing energy is taken to other dimensions of The Infinite Spirit.

I write so that you will question, examine and recognize "What's Really Going On"!

I write because I love and respect you. You are a part of me as I am a part of you.

I have been through many trials and tribulations as you probably have also. Wake Up Call One exposes the dimensions that I have explored and experienced. It exposes my perspective. I want you to explore my perspective and put it in your brain rolodex of anything's possible. It is so very important to explore other perspectives. It is so very important to examine and evaluate those perspectives.

I asked a question: "Why do people prefer hate over love"? The Infinite Spirit heard me and took me on all kinds of explorations and experiences to other dimensions. I was awakened to some of what's really going on.

Know that there will always be more to explore and experience because the Infinite Spirit is infinitely creating.

The Infinite Spirit showed me that all and everything are off-springs originating from The Infinite Spirit. We are of the same energy and have shattered into infinite pieces. We travel in the same and or different dimensions. We carry different covers exuding and spouting the same and or different perspectives, thoughts and essence of The Infinite Spirit. We are able to explore and experience all dimensions created by The Infinite Spirit.

The Upper Dimensions of The Infinite Spirit are those dimensions that you are led to believe you will explore and experience when you die. Wrong! You are able to explore and experience them now. They are non-judgmental dimensions, unconditional love dimensions, recognizing what's really going on dimensions and "Ultimate Respect" dimensions!

The Christ Dimension is a part of The Infinite Spirit's Upper Dimensions and resides in your Spirit. In order to recognize and release your programming, you must awaken you—your Spirit from hibernation so that you will awaken your Christ Dimension. When your Christ Dimension is awakened, you recognize that you–your Spirit is a Child of The Infinite Spirit and that you must give you "Ultimate Respect"! The Spirit, Jesus of Nazareth spoke the words and showed the ways to follow to awaken your Christ Dimension. As a result of his teachings, I awakened my Christ Dimension and now explore and experience the Upper Dimensions of The Infinite Spirit.

The Lower Dimensions of The Infinite Spirit are dimensions consisting of programming which hide your Spirit from your awareness. They are dimensions that you must explore and experience to develop your Spirit. You must go through a series of lessons, situations, potholes or tests which, at some point, will awaken you to the truths of reality and to what's really going on. You must fill your Spirit with strength, patience, love and knowledge while exploring and experiencing in these lower dimensions.

The programming breeds dimensions of hell enveloped with confusion and mesmerizing illusions. They are dimensions spouting disrespect, madness and chaos enabling the conformists to keep you in these programming dimensions longer than necessary thereby, delaying your ultimate purpose. The energy of these programming dimensions works to keep you—your physical body in charge of you—your Spirit. These programming dimensions work to keep all of you in bondage. All your self-destructive notions and habits originate from the programming. It is imperative that you are always aware of who you are and whose you are. This is necessary to know before you are able to continue your journeys into other dimensions of The Infinite Spirit. Wake Up Call One will enlighten you to the programming orchestrated in the lower dimensions on planet Earth.

Your Spirit is infinite. Your existence is on-going whether on planet Earth or out of planet Earth. Your Spirit will not always travel in a physical body as you are now. Your time on planet Earth is not long. Oh yes! You may live to be one hundred years or more but, this is very short compared to the age a Spirit lived on planet Earth before pollution, corrosion, ingesting over the counter, prescription and illegal drugs, inhaling cigarettes, drinking alcohol and experimentation with human Spirits.

You are always learning. As a Spirit of The Infinite Spirit, you have free will to choose which dimensions you want to explore and experience. Seek other perspectives; for other Spirits may have explored, experienced and awakened to perspectives you may not know about. We learn from all these different perspectives.

You have an affect on other Spirits who will, in turn, have an affect on more Spirits. You have the capability to be where you want to be and unless you awaken, like, accept, love and respect your Spirit, you will not recognize or use those capabilities. You limit your abilities when you think only inside the box. It is imperative that you know and respect your Spirit. This you must do for you!

View all things with an open mind and unbiased. Examine all information received from all venues. Examine all words that come your way. Examine all ways that may want to stay as the only way. Examine everything closely before wholeheartedly accepting its concept thoroughly. Question! Question! Question! Learn from all of The Infinite Spirit!

The knowing of your Spirit is very important
Recognize who your Spirit really is
Recognize that your Spirit is you and you alone
Recognize how powerful you are
Recognize that your creativity is unlimited

You must know who you are
To the depths of your core
You must also know that
The way you are raised in this programming
Molds your physical body to a programmed mode of operation
You are programmed to be against your own Spirit

To do as the conformists' programming dictates
You follow unbalanced programming
Causing you to contribute to the programming dimensions of madness

Man against woman
Woman against man
Man against man
Woman against woman
All against children

Wake Up Call One is a wake up call to awaken your Spirit from hibernation and recognize what's really going on!

This is not a cult. This is my perspective! Just as Bishop Thomas D. Jakes, Senator Barack Obama, Oprah, Dr Bill Winston, Dr. Cornell West, Joseph Campbell, Bill Moyers, etc., etc., etc. give you their perspective, this is my perspective. This is what I have learned. This is my dissertation for my doctorate. This is my philosophy from The Infinite Spirit. I give you another twist of "What's Really Going On"!

The Infinite Spirit is calling for your Spirit reconnection. You are the teachers. Children are watching you. They are learning from you. What are you teaching them? Are you guiding them to reconnect with The Infinite Spirit?

There are many ways to recognize what's really going on. You have a plethora of lies to reveal. Unveil the truths in the lies which are programming your Spirit to explore and experience only in the programming. Pray for strength and guidance; for the essences of your truths will change as your Spirit awakening increases. Pray for recognition of "What's Really Going On"!

As you are reading and or listening to my words, know that I felt you reading and listening as I was writing or saying this to you. May you explore and experience the wonderfulness of The Infinite Spirit!

You do not have the definitive answers
And I do not have the definitive answers
But, if we get together and look at all the perspective answers
That means we get closer and closer to the definitive answers
We need to talk and evaluate
Let us put our genius together and
Address the matters at hand
Let us stamp out this oil greed
Let us reverse these wars which are killing our children
Let us take action regarding global warming
We need to talk

Know that in our meetings
We are gathered as Spirits of The Infinite Spirit
Spirits who will effectuate solutions
To benefit other Spirits
These solutions will also benefit planet Earth as a whole
We are gathered here open minded
Seeing all perspectives as having merit
We will combine these perspectives
Fine tune them
We will effectuate solutions to expose
The programming dimensions of madness
We are gathered here as Family
Not as leaders
For every one of us is a leader
Our Spirits spawned by
The Infinite Spirit of All That Is
We will effectuate solutions that will benefit
All of our family of Spirits and
Planet Earth as a whole
Family is important
We are Family!

Jehovah Sharma!

The Infinite Spirit's

Presence Is Here!

Hallelujah!

CHAPTER ONE

BEGINNING

Know that Everything originates from
The Infinite Spirit

The Infinite Spirit exploded
Splitting infinitely
Creating infinite dimensions to explore and experience
The Infinite Spirit activated planet Earth
Awakening her planted seeds of life filled with
Energy blowing breaths of concentrated spirituality to catch and inhale
The birthing of these new seeds bring forth Spirits who come to
Explore and experience
All Dimensions of The Infinite Spirit

Where are you without planet Earth? Planet Earth gives us the necessary essentials to live in this planetary dimension. We were given dominion over planet Earth meaning we take care of her and love her to a high degree. Love planet Earth for she originates from The Infinite Spirit!

Know that the programming dimensions are prominent on planet Earth and disrespect every Spirit ... disrespect everything. Know that every Spirit and everything originates from the Infinite Spirit!

Release that disrespect! Replace it with "Ultimate Respect"!

Awaken! Awaken! Awaken!

Who are you?
You are a miracle
You inherit The Infinite Spirit's explorations and experiences
You are good and bad
You are love and hate
You are happiness and sadness
You are forgiving and anger
You must awaken and recognize that
You-your Spirit is a Child of The Infinite Spirit!

The conformists have you believing that
You are the scum of planet Earth and
Need constant improvement
Come back to reality
Right now
You are exploring and experiencing

Programming dimensions of fantasylands
Illusions breeding lies
The conformists who choose to implement and
Enforce the programming dimensions
Are Spirits of The Infinite Spirit
Playing with Pinocchio and stuff in the
Programming dimensions of madness which are filled with
Hate … hurt … anger … depression
Among many other forms of madness
Programming dimensions where your fantasies grow bigger and bigger
Become your reality
Become your dimensions of destruction

Wake Up Call! It's A Wake Up Call Y'all!

CHAPTER TWO

INTRO

All Praises to The Infinite Spirit!

I was putting words together in 2001 for the purpose of recording them on CD and to speak and perform them on stage. I was setting up to implement my purpose which is to help other Spirits awaken to what's really going on! But, June 10, 2003 had other plans for my dreams. There was more I had to learn and more preparation needed.

I was reviewing those words today, March 2, 2007 and discovered that I wanted to put my original format in this book. So, here goes my final retech (Authorhouse's term) or my final version of my first book.

One more thing, if any musician out there feels my words with music then, let's put our genius together and release a slam dunk CD!

Here it is folks ...

"The Spoken Book" Part One

Whaaasuuup my Spirits? My name is Wake Up Call Y'all
I expose the games you need to know
In order to survive and become independent
You are part of this show that goes on
Day to day ... year to year ... century to century
That causes you to shed too many a tear
You don't have to suffer as they say you do
You are strong and mighty ...
A child of The Infinite Spirit
Your spirits will be replenished
To see your accomplishments of many goals

Wake Up Call ... It's A Wake Up Call Y'all!

Now, get comfortable and CHILL!
Ride with the glide.

Awaken ... Awaken ... Awaken!

Set forth in America in the 1700's and
Who knows how many centuries before this time
Were these same principles being taught to human Spirits
For the sake of control
The programming dimensions were heavily carried out by Willie Lynch
One among many others

He was a Caucasian slave owner in the West Indies
Hired by American slave owners
To show them how to make a slave
This programming targeted a specific group of people but,
Know that it eventually includes all people

These programming dimensions you are subjected to while learning how to be a human being need to be identified and broken!

Iyanla Van Zant says
You feel to the marrow of your bones
This is where your programming is sitting right now
In the marrow of your bones
Absorbing into your blood
Giving you diseases
Cancers
Viruses
Making you sick and tired of being sick and tired of being sick and tired
Keeping you angry
Causing you to be severely unstable in the programming dimensions

You must clean and readjust your marrow! Think deeply on this for this is so very important! You must break the programming saturating all of your flesh!

Wake Up Call! ... It's A Wake Up Call Y'all!

Awaken ... Awaken ... Awaken!

You are in a time of a great awakening of all people
An awakening that will reunite us all as
The Children ... the Spirits of The Infinite Spirit
The truth prevails for the healing of the masses of adults and children lost

The children ... Oh the children are so lost in the programming dimensions of madness! We must help them find their way out of these programming dimensions of madness!

Know that all of these dimensions were created by The Infinite Spirit
Know that these programming dimensions are what folks see as hell
Oh yeah! It's hell alright!

Hell is necessary to wake you up!

You have to go through hell to reconnect to heaven
The truth will give way to "What's Really Going On"!

We have beautiful children who are Spirits of The Infinite Spirit
Being born every day
They deserve a wonderful life of
Marvelous explorations and experiences
They are not experiencing that now!

We teach the words of truths and lies for all to see!

Children do not understand about the consequences of
Their thoughts and actions ...
Their lies and
Therefore, they do things without forethought
Children should be taught about the programming and
The disrespect it advocates
First and foremost
It is up to us to ensure that they awaken

Awaken their Spirit and give their Spirit **"Ultimate Respect"**!

AWAKEN Spirits to the TRUTH of the GAMES!

AWAKEN Spirits to the TRUTH of the LIES!

AWAKEN Spirits to the TRUTH of the HATE!

You find the truth in all religions ... all philosophies ... all perspectives
You find the truth in all things that are of The Infinite Spirit!

AWAKEN YOUR HIBERNATING SPIRIT!

Celebrate your life!
Recognize the miracles of you!
Awaken your magnificent self!
These are wonderful times!
You will make a big difference!
Rejoice!

Wake Up Call! It's A Wake Up Call Y'all!

9

CHAPTER THREE

SWEET LIFE BEGINS

You–your Spirit is energy
Whose composition is made up of atoms
Of which their basic composition is
Protons, neutrons, and electrons
Filled with positive, negative and motivational charges
Know that you are a miracle
A beautiful miracle
You are a part of energy released from The Infinite Spirit
A thought freed to create its own thoughts
Explore its own dimensions
While still being a part of
The Infinite Creation
When you look at you
When you look at another human Spirit
An animal
A tree
A rock
The ocean
Anything and everything
You gaze upon ...
All energy on planet Earth
In the universe
The galaxies
And beyond
You gaze at a manifestation of
The Infinite Spirit
Miracles!
Wonderfully beautiful miracles!

It's the sperm
The sperm that started it all
The sperm y'all
You rode in on the wave of a sperm from a male physical body
Injected into the womb of a female physical body

You are the sperm
The sperm that formed the egg that hatched your Spirit
Your Spirit sparked the life
While riding on the wave of a sperm from a male physical body
Injected into the womb of a female physical body
You traveled through many dimensions
On the way to your development

You sparked the sperm
The sperm that bore no germ
Until you hit the terra firm
After you came to term

You sparked the sperm
As you were riding … riding
Just cruising … cruising
Surfing on the wave of a sperm
That's you y'all
From beginning to end
Top to bottom
Know who you are

You are Spirit originating from The Infinite Spirit!

Oh yes!
You are Spirit
Who rode in on the wave of a sperm
Injected into the womb
A fleeing warm proton joining with a neutron
Electrons energize
Substance clings to your naked Spirit as
You find a comfortable place to rest
From the exhilarating journey
Your shape is forming
Organs take their place
Relegating physical gender establishment
The warmth is stimulating

You are a Spirit spawned by The Infinite Spirit
Ever-changing
Ever-growing
Ever-learning
Alas!
The breath of freedom has arrived
You are a miracle again!
Waaaahhhhhhh! Waaaahhhhhhh! Waaaahhhhhhh!

"It's a wonderful, healthy baby"! The doctor said. "Look how beautiful"!
(A main introduction to the programming)

"Never mind how beautiful I am"! I said. "Put some clothes on me. I am freezing! Hey Mom … when do I eat"?

But, no one was listening.

The first words you should hear after being born are

YOU ARE SPIRIT

ORIGINATING FROM

THE INFINITE SPIRIT

How is a baby a sinner upon birth?
A sinner, y'all!
The Clergy say that you are born into sin
I learned that
You are first touched by programming dimensions
Where sin is promoted

They were preaching God is love
And breeding hate to the highest
They were preaching thou shalt not commit adultery
Thou shalt not be gay
And raping little boys and girls
They were faithful on Sunday
Filthy on Monday through Saturday
Contradictions, hypocrisy and hell fire
They were America's finest
They were followers of Jesus

15

They were followers of the Star of David
They were followers of the Koran
They were followers of Buddha, etc., etc., etc.
They were the blind leading the blind
Into the dens of inequity

One becomes a sinner because
Your Spirit entry into the physical body
Takes you to the programming dimensions of The Infinite Spirit
Sin is promoted by the programming dimensions
Which train you to choose to explore and thereby experience
The programming dimensions of madness only

Your so-called moralistic teachings and values
Emanate from programming dimensions of lies
Your first teachings come from parents
Who are usually God-fearing and
Deeply immersed into these programming dimensions
They struggle so much
Feeling so good about their business life
While overlooking and forgetting about
Their personal life
Forgetting their families
Forgetting their children
Forgetting their love
Becoming lost in the programming dimensions of madness

Wake Up Call! It's A Wake Up Call Y'all!

CHAPTER FOUR

LET THE PROGRAM BEGIN

They made you believe
You were crazy
They wanted control over you
They made you believe
You were evil ... the devil's child
They wanted control ... they wanted control over your Spirit

Your first taste of control, discipline, and pain
In this plane of existence
Is the cutting of your cord
And the slap on your bottom ever to remain
They must see if you are normal ...
If your flesh responds to their first ebbs of programming
The possession of your cord begins

You are programmed to be normal as normal is taught
By self-designated Spirits wanting
To be lords and masters over other Spirits
You think designated thoughts
And react with designated actions
That use designated definitions
For words used in designated thoughts

This programming represents unnatural thinking, acting and feeling
Giving illusions of independence
While one reaps total dependence
Loss of Spirit control
Unbalanced thinking
Allowing only your physical body to be in charge
Leaving you with one third of the truth

> Your purpose for being becomes lost in programming dimensions of
> Rules and regulations

They made you believe
You were crazy
They wanted control over you
They made you believe
You were evil ... the devil's child
They wanted control ... they wanted control over your Spirit

Your Spirit is growing
You are breathing and functioning

Mom takes you home
Puts you into a room by yourself
You look at bars
While sucking from a bottle propped upon a pillow
With toys surrounding every inch of your body
Your Spirit yearning for Spirit emotion and caring
Becomes an unnatural expose of material substitutions
That expose becomes an accepted way of receiving because
YOU ARE not aware …
YOU ARE NOT aware …
You are NOT AWARE of
Any other concept or teaching
Your Spirit is being programmed to desire
Material things

Ages zero to thirteen are the indelible learning years
One inhales all knowledge … all energy surrounding
The programming appeals to your physical body
Your Spirit is disrespected … lost … helpless
Your Spirit is monitored and evaluated
Through good and bad thoughts and actions
Guilty or not guilty
Saint or devil

There is wonderful attention when you are good
"Ooooo! What a sweet child you are … I love you"!

There is ugly, abusive attention when you are bad
"You are so stupid! Get out of my sight"!

The love is either or
Developing into a love of habit … not heart

Your Spirit sense falls prey to pledging allegiance
To the programming dimensions of right and wrong
YOUR aware thoughts are shaped …
Your AWARE THOUGHTS are shaped …
Your aware thoughts are SHAPED
For programming ideologies of friendship, love and disrespect
Your physical body is being prepared to take control and
Keep your Spirit in bondage

"Conform"! They say. "Look up, pray and obey you sinners"!

They made you believe
You were crazy
They wanted control over you
They made you believe
You were evil ... the devil's child
They wanted control ... they wanted control over your Spirit

You survive potty training and
Learn basic words
As the lead of your pencil outlines A, B, C, D
Your time has come for hard-core confusing indoctrination
Religion comes into focus
Your Spirit feels its connection to The Infinite Spirit
You identify this connection with fear

"Do as you are told or the wrath of God will be upon you"!

A stage is set to open your Spirit to concentrate wholly on
The programming dimensions and their pitfalls
To love, honor and obey is firm and planted

You leave one dimension
Of do and don'ts
To go to dimensions
Of stricter do and don'ts
Only some of these
Do and don'ts
Go against
The do and don'ts
You just learned
"What's Really Going On"?

Your awareness sees you as a sinner
Trying to like, accept, love and respect your Spirit with
A programming attitude
Dimensions of confusion arise
You are on your way to a nightmarish venture into
The shaping of your Spirit

They made you believe you were nothing and never would be nothing
more than nothing!

You are given a glimmer of hope and
Allowed the privilege of atoning for your sins but,

The programming advocates that
You will always be a sinner
Your awareness of your Spirit connection with The Infinite Spirit
Becomes inundated with programming temptations
This is the ways, lies and disrespect
Your chances of being at one with The Infinite Spirit are
Zero to nothing
A strange and shameful type of energy penetrates your Spirit
The programming of your physical body is winning as
Your Spirit submits, becomes docile and
Comfortable with exploring and experiencing
The programming dimensions of madness

They made you believe
You were crazy
They wanted control over you
They made you believe
You were evil … the devil's child
They wanted control … they wanted control over your Spirit

It's all a part of the programming dimensions
The perpetrating
The games
The madness

The programming says you are no good
Insane
Loco
And, who you been talkin' to

The programming gains complete control of your Spirit
Control of
The way you talk
The way you walk
The way you think
Control of your every move
Your Spirit is taken and left on a bad groove

It's the programming y'all
The lying
The cheating
The hating

Superficial joy
Superficial friendship
Superficial love
Your Spirit is hated
Your demise is plotted

The programming says,

"Through you-your physical body, I control you-your Spirit! I abuse you-your physical body and you-your Spirit"!

So! You know what I say,

Wake up! Wake up! Wake up!

"May The Infinite Spirit be your walk ... your talk ... your love"!

All Praises to The Infinite Spirit!

You are aware of the horrors of life
Awaken Spirits
To the beauty of life
You are aware of the hates of life
Awaken Spirits
To the loves of life
Regenerate your Spirit awareness
Yo woman
Hey man
Do you see what's really going on?

Oh yes! You are in a game
To be sure
It is not about paranoia
It is real
It is alive and well
After you see the purpose
Of the programming dimensions
You will see that
You must wake up now
Oh yes!
You are in a game
To be sure
You Better Recognize!

They made you believe
You were crazy
They wanted control over you
They made you believe
You were evil … the devil's child
They wanted control … they wanted control over your Spirit

School days, school days
Dear old golden rule days

The pain of permanent teeth is forgotten as
You concentrate on grammar school
You are an excellent prospect for becoming totally conformed
You follow every rule … every word
Wanting to be perfect in your learning
You receive constant praise
Pride abounds

The programming has your undivided attention
As your Spirit is silently programmed to
Respond to physical body programming beckoning …

Stand in line
No talking
No chewing gum
No talking back
No eating
No smiling
No, no, no
You do as we tell you
You believe what
We want you to believe
We are in control of you

"No problem"! You say. "I don't want to be like those sinners! It is my natural instinct to learn. Mama told me that you are the experts who know what I am to learn. Show me more of how I should be! I want to be a good citizen"!

Teacher attention is less at high school
The demands of home are resented
Textbook nurturing becomes excessively rigid
Your aware thoughts, instincts and respect

Are accepting scholarly thoughts, instincts, and disrespect with enthusiasm
While programming dimensions of
Hate, anger, jealousy, hurt, etc., etc., etc.
Possess and control your Spirit
You are conforming
But deeply resisting
Your aspirations of being so called perfectly normal are smashed
Your Spirit hopes
Become stripped and left for death
You succumb to prisons of
Programming thoughts and ideology
You watch your friends participate in their graduation ceremony
Honoring their achievements of totally losing
Their Spirit respect
There they are ...
Success stories in the great volumes of programming dimensions' history

And then, there are those who escaped the halls of programming history and
Took a test of textbook ideology
Passed and received their G.E.D
No caps
No gowns
No ceremonies
No history and
Left in the low ends of the programming dimensions of madness

They made you believe
You were crazy
They wanted control over you
They made you believe
You were evil ... the devil's child
They wanted control ... they wanted control over your Spirit

"Okay! I'm an adult now"!

You pack your suitcase and leave
Your parents' house to be responsible for yourself
You seek to live happily ever after with lots of money

"Okay! On my own! Free to do what I want! I am ready for it all"!

Your knowledge of what is out there for you to experience
Is minimal
Your awareness of being in a programmed mode
Is nil
You are a child
Trying to tackle and survive
The programming dimensions of fantasies, games and lies
You explore and experience programming dimensions of
Believing you know about real life
You find fairy tale love
Vicious greediness
And oh so much hate

"Eighteen years old ... single ... one child. I need a job. I have no skills".

You become stereotyped
Categorized for low class labor
You accept a minimum wage job
Your 'so called' intelligence did not quite make
The programming's grade of perfection
You did not learn well enough
To reap the privileges and rewards of the programming dimensions
You are not worthy of the riches
But, you qualify for welfare from the
Programming dimensions that will hopefully
Mend your non-conforming Spirit

Whether or not you have gone on to college
Or work minimum wage jobs
You are exploring and experiencing the programming dimensions
To think and act as you were and or are told
An enslaved clone

A lot of your programming
Comes from the educational system
Preparing you to function
For the business way of life
Teaching you the laws of money which is
The foundation that keeps you mesmerized ... dedicated
Attentively immersed in the programming dimensions
Which encompass your entire physical body

As you willingly accept all the madness

I ask you,

"What is leading you ... your Spirit or your physical body"?

They made you believe
You were crazy
They wanted control over you
They made you believe
You were evil ... the devil's child
They wanted control ... they wanted control over your Spirit

There you are
A captured spirit
Bathing in programming dimensions
Your Spirit explores and experiences
Countless programming dimensions of madness
Your Spirit is
Kicked
Torn
Tattered
Raped
Shredded
Molded
Suppressed

You are a mess!

You become confused
You feel abnormal
Disrespected
Alone
Unloved
You ignore your responsibility to
You and your family

Do you know what's really going on?

A state of depression invades your sanity
Your energy becomes flaccid and diminished
You are unable to connect any dots
There is just too much to remember
To think and act according to programming expectations

Your Spirit has lost its connection to The Infinite Spirit
You yearn for escape from
The nagging and oh so pressing obligations
You want to escape the shame
The 'so called' failures
You are running scared
But there is no where to run ...
No where to hide

"There has to be something better! My life has to have some meaning"!

You search frantically for answers
You hold fast to thoughts that
There will be happiness for you
What to do ... what to do?

Examine your thoughts
Examine your actions
Listen to other perspectives
Open your awareness
Listen to answers emanating from everywhere
Learn that anything's possible

All Praises To The Infinite Spirit!

Do you swear to yourself that you always tell the truth, while telling your children to lie and say you are not at home if bill collectors or someone you do not want to talk with calls you? Then, do you have the nerve to chastise your children severely when they lie to you?

Do you break commitments to you and other Spirits? Do you become puzzled when other Spirits break commitments to you?

Has your job become your freedom where you are wonderfully pleasant to all? Has your home become a prison where no one can do anything right, including you?

Are you controlled by the programming dimensions of madness? Are you sabotaging your living moments?

"What's Really Going On"?

Fantasies of perfection

Always out of reach
Do you see that
You are a miracle
Not liking, accepting, loving or respecting
Any part of you-your Spirit
Who is ignored ... imprisoned
Do you see that
You are a miracle
Who deserves the best of everything

We are like seeds that bear fruit
Seeds opening doors to other possibilities
Doors to other dimensions
The experiences of every Spirit
Are important
No matter how mundane they appear to be
They are all doors that
Lead to the Infinite Dimensions
Of The Infinite Spirit
Right now, you are exploring and experiencing
The Infinite Spirit's programming dimensions of madness

Read on and live your moments to the maximum! Take new information and examine it carefully before accepting it. All perspectives are important.

Wake Up Call! It's A Wake Up Call Y'all!

CHAPTER FIVE

WE BEGIN YOUR AWAKENING

Awake

Not sleeping or lethargic
Roused from sleep
Vigilant
Alert
To cease to sleep
Come out of sleep or a sleep like state
Give new life to
Stir up

Aware

Aware usually implies vigilance in observing or in drawing inferences
from what one sees, hears, etc.
Sensible implies the operation of something like a sixth sense
Alive adds to sensible the implication of acute sensitiveness to something
Awake implies that one has become alive to something and is on alert
Cognizant implies special or certain knowledge
Conscious implies awareness of something when one allows it to enter his
mind and usually fixes his attention upon it
Apprised
Informed

Ultimate

Beyond which nothing is contemplated or intended
That concludes, process, course of action or series
No longer alterable
Definitive
The final point or result
The end
The last step

Respect

To regard, consider, take into account
To pay attention to
To observe carefully
To treat or regard with deference, esteem or honor
To prize
To value

To treat with consideration
To refrain from interfering with
To expect
To anticipate
To look at
To face

Dimension

The action of measuring
Measurable extent of any kind as the length, breadth, height, magnitude, thickness and volume
A term for the (unknown or variable) quantities contained in any product as factors
Any power of a quantity being of the dimensions denoted by its index
The number of dimensions corresponds to the degree of a quantity or equation

AWAKEN YOUR HIBERNATING SPIRIT …

AWAKEN YOUR MAGNIFICENT SPIRIT

SEE THE MIRACLES OF YOU!

If we could just see
That we are all connected
That what affects one
Affects the other to infinity

If we could just see
That this programming energy
That people are thinking, saying and doing
Has become the predominate energy

If we could just see
That this energy has
Put planet Earth and her inhabitants
In a state of gross imbalance

You are the new generations
Who have a task to do
Do not think that because your ancestors
Made it easier for you
To reach the accolades of the business world
That you can just lay back
And collect a fat paycheck
Oh no!
I am sorry to ruin your dreams of laziness
For to rid this nation and other nations of injustices
Bestowed upon all human Spirits
You have a great battle to fight

Greater than your strong, elegant, dedicated, persevering and loving ancestors fought!

Yours is a task of bringing forth
The new age
Bringing forth the days of peace
You must be prepared
Be prepared for the upcoming wars
About to be waged
Actually,
It is going pretty strong right now
Peace will be accomplished when
All Spirits awaken

Your Spirit calls to be recognized and known! Your existence is meaningful! You are alive! Freedom awaits your Spirit! Become aware of your ignorance. Become aware of love. Become aware, for you have found someone to love ... YOUR SPIRIT! Who are you? Do you know? "You Better Recognize"!

Be aware of
Who and what is controlling your Spirit
You must know who you are
From the beginning of you
To have full awareness of your Spirit
That is when you started your explorations and experiences
In this plane of existence
That is when you started learning
The programming in
The Lower Dimensions of The Infinite Spirit

35

From the moment you start having thoughts about liking, accepting, loving and respecting your Spirit, you will start having thoughts which will awaken your Spirit.

Wake Up Call! It's A Wake Up Call Y'all!

CHAPTER SIX

AWARE THOUGHTS ARE MOST IMPORTANT!

WHEN YOU THINK

YOU CREATE WHAT YOU THINK!

Aware thoughts are so important. You must recognize their importance. Aware thoughts are amazing! When you think, a piece of your Spirit energy leaves your physical body and creates the what, when, where, who, why and how of your thoughts. All of this your Spirit does by your aware thoughts. These are most important reasons for being aware of whom your Spirit is and recognizing whether or not your Spirit is being respected. Spirits are held in bondage because they are not aware of the power of their aware thoughts which are Infinite Spirit connected. If your aware thoughts live in programming dimensions of paranoia and fear, then you create those dimensions to return and affect your Spirit.

Aware thoughts in a programming sense
De-energize motivation
Stagnate growth
Create a death
Especially of those things promoting life
Death merely means a change to another form
The programming death to your Spirit
Changes your potential of unlimited knowledge
Your programming dimensions of thinking
Controls your Spirit
Which in turn
Creates death of your Spirit aware thinking
Which in turn
Creates a Spirit who does not care about her or his Spirit
A Spirit who does not care about her or his protection
Originating from The Infinite Spirit
This in turn
Creates death of your exploring and experiencing in
All the dimensions of The Infinite Spirit

Your Spirit, which is surrounded by your physical body, is remarkable! One of your auras[1] extends two to three feet from your physical body. It may be more depending upon your Spirit awareness and connection to The Infinite Spirit. The projection of your Spirit lessens when you are mesmerized by the programming.

---

[1] The Aura, W.E. Butler

39

Other Spirit energy will affect you in many ways. Become aware of as many ways as possible. Have you ever noticed how sometimes your mood can change so quickly? You are having a great time, in a great mood, in walks someone and BLAM! You have entered into programming dimensions of anger, hurt, etc., etc., etc. and your great feeling is a thing of the past. Your attitude becomes ugly, rude, sarcastic ... just downright mean! What the heck happened? What brought you to hell again? Whose programming thoughts influenced you?

Thoughts travel ad infinitum, through many dimensions, many Spirits and many things leaving and adding a little of the dimensions of those thoughts in all the people, places and things they come in contact with. Powerful and creative energy charges are released through your thoughts. A lot of the dimensions of thoughts which surround you are some other Spirit's programming dimensions of thoughts. A part of your Spirit energy and other Spirit energy linger for awhile in all the places you walk and in all the chairs you sit. Some thoughts just float through you. Some thoughts cling to you and you end up absorbing their programming dimensions of unhappiness, hate, pain, etc., etc., etc.

If the thoughts of another Spirit pass through you, you absorb and experience the dimensions of thoughts they are in. Whenever you are near anyone, you absorb their energy and they absorb yours. It is through that absorption that you read and or feel the energies of their Spirit thoughts and feelings. Your Spirit reads and or feels where they were and are. Your Spirit reads and or feels what they are thinking. This is also how a child acquires habits from parents and others surrounding them without verbalization or visualization. They read and or feel their unbalanced programming dimensions of thinking and acting. They read and or feel their disconnected Spirit. When you know your Spirit, you will rid your Spirit and your body of your dimensions of programming and other Spirits' dimensions of programming that you have absorbed.

What about Spirit connected thoughts? You are affected by Spirit connected thoughts also but, the emitting of Spirit connected thoughts is very slight because the dimensions of programming have become dominant thereby silencing its affect. When one dimension of energy overpowers another, the aware thoughts and actions submit to that dominance.

Spirits projecting programming thoughts
Will cause you to experience dimensions of
Aches
Pains
Mood swings
Without your Spirit being aware that
You are being or have been invaded
By harmful thoughts
Threatening your Spirit connection to The Infinite Spirit

You must examine your thoughts to insure that they are the thoughts you want to have. Listen to your thoughts because they do tell you if something is right or wrong and will it or will it not be of benefit to you. Recognize where your thoughts and knowledge are coming from. Refrain from accepting any type of information instantly. Think about everything before you accept it. Know that belief should not be seen as absolute. There is a possibility that your beliefs may have to be changed for the betterment of your Spirit. The more knowledge you acquire, the more your beliefs will be taken to other levels and therefore, will have to be changed.

Free your Spirit from the imprisonment of
Your programming dimensions of thoughts and actions

Your Spirit thoughts are the keys to your kingdoms ... inner and outer. Your worries would not affect your living if you recognized the power of your Spirit thoughts. Your thoughts determine whether you merely survive and exist or fully survive and live. Your Spirit thoughts will take you anywhere you want to be. This is how you have unlimited capabilities. All things are possible through your Spirit thoughts ... the new saying for this is all things are possible supernaturally. You--your physical body is limited. You--your Spirit is unlimited. Your thoughts will give it all ... your thoughts will take it all. It is amazing! It is a miracle! It is what you think it is! Do you know your Spirit thoughts?

Wake Up Call! It's A Wake Up Call Y'all!

CHAPTER SEVEN

CHANGE IS INEVITABLE

You explore ... you experience and
With each exploration and experience
There are lessons to learn
Wisdom to gain
Each time you change your thinking and your actions
You start new and wonderful adventures
Into other dimensions of The Infinite Spirit
Reach for the exciting dimensions
Reach for the marvelous dimensions
Reach for the Upper Dimensions of The Infinite Spirit

One of the reasons for Spirits to be together is to help each other get through the changes and the deaths which are experienced daily and moment to moment. The melancholy, the worries and the pits are the programming dimensions of madness we all endure. You need a best friend at these times. Be that best friend to you and others.

Change is delightful and frightening
Change means growth
Forget the disappointments of the past
Remember the lessons of the past
Reconnect to the everlasting energy that created us all!

Do not be afraid
Release those heavy bonds of habit that are
Manifested in the programming dimensions which
Interfere with your confidence that
You have established for your Spirit
The intensity will penetrate and
Affect your arrangement of energy within
Your Spirit and take you out of your change

Feel wonderful about changing you to
The way you want to be
Change gives you another chance to
Live without the programming
Go to accomplish!
Change is inevitable!

The moment your balance starts
Descending to imbalance
Is the moment your confidence starts dwindling

Starts changing back to before the change
Your thoughts return to programming dimensions
Rendering a vulnerability
Allowing the resurfacing of
Programming thoughts that
Regain your concentrated attention
Wake up to see that your change has changed
Pay attention
Recognize the dimensions you are in

Wake Up Call! It's A Wake Up Call Y'all!

CHAPTER EIGHT

LET'S CHECK OUT THIS PROGRAMMING!

Programming

To arrange or furnish a program of or for
To enter in a program

You better recognize which dimensions
You are exploring and experiencing

All the hurt ... all the hate originating from the programming dimensions
Made you lose your pretty
Made you lose your innocence
Made you lose your connection to The Infinite Spirit
Made you become the hate that hurts

The programming dimensions cause you to lose your naked pretty
Lose your naked innocence and
Clothe it with hate
Anger
Jealousy
Lust and
Disrespect
A few mentioned among many, many other uglies

A new perspective is needed to awaken those stuck in the old perspective originating from the programming dimensions.

They took your pretty and
Mangled it to cold void
Feeling like a slump of just here and
Not liking it here

They took your pretty with
Their insults and ridicules and humiliations and lies and judgments and
Just downright nastiness

They took your pretty
They took your fearlessness
They took your aware connection to The Infinite Spirit
They took your Spirit and
Dipped it in hot water and
Abandoned you and
Left you in the hands of a rapist
They took your pretty

They took your pretty and
Under the name of greed
They left you homeless and hungry

They led you to
The abyss of the pits
They took your pretty and
Turned you into sinners and
Killers and
Pessimists and
Angry Spirits and
Haters

They took your pretty to
The programming dimensions of madness

When did they take your pretty?

Your Spirit instincts of life and their intentions are surrealistically taken through camouflaged programming. You grow up thinking that the programming ideology gives you a balanced life. You follow step by step through all the expected and unexpected stages and your Spirit soon loses all sense of freedom to think independently. You hire psychiatrists and or psychologists or consult books set up by the conformists on how and what to think. These books are great. Know that they address you—your physical body. Your Spirit is not even talked about. You will learn in a programmed mode but, it is only the dimensions that the conformists want you to learn. These dimensions exclude your independence and respect of your Spirit. Your Spirit is imprisoned. You do not even realize that there are other dimensions to explore and experience.

You are stuck because
You were programmed to be dependent
Dependent upon the programming of the flesh
It started with Adam and Eve
That is when a Spirit of The Infinite Spirit
Stumbled into
The Infinite Spirit's dimensions of programming
It was then that
The Upper Dimensions of The Infinite Spirit
Were shut out
From all Spirits
It was then that man thought he could take the place of The Infinite
Spirit
Hiding your Spirit connection to

The Infinite Spirit
Hiding your nakedness
Replacing it with shame
Hiding your innocence
Replacing it with guilt
Hiding the protection of
The Infinite Spirit
Hiding the love of
The Infinite Spirit
Hiding half of The Infinite Spirit
Know that the programming dimensions of madness are
Just other dimensions of
The Infinite Spirit

The programming coerces you to play games which you have difficulty mastering because you are a Child of The Infinite Spirit. You play these games which encourage and force you to go against The Infinite Spirit's Laws you instinctively know but, were programmed not to pay attention to. You are enticed to break programming laws and The Infinite Spirit's Laws every day and think nothing of it.

Why are Spirits not following any of these Laws? Spirits are disconnected from The Infinite Spirit. They follow conformist Spirits who are teaching and preaching their perspective formed by the programming. You work with double standards, exceptions and guilt. Guilt sets up thoughts of punishment, whereby, the human Spirit is programmed to automatically set up punishment for its Spirit.

Very few see the truth. Most are blind because of programming dimensions which were absorbed at an early age. These dimensions carry programming knowledge on a mundane level teaching one perspective which retards and limits Spirit growth. One side of the brain carries the weight as opposed to both sides of the brain[3] working together, i.e. right and left energies working in harmony. For example, it is the same principle that can be applied to two spirits together when they do not work together. Not only have their thoughts and actions become left-brained but their relationship also becomes left-brained or regimented holding programming dimensions of fear, jealousy and pain which breed dependency and hate. Your friendships are buried and your right brain is shut out. The Spirit becomes mute. All is unbalanced when one perspective is heeded.

---

[3] Writing on Both Sides of the Brain, Henriette Anne Klauser

The programming takes away all your Spirit connections
The substitution is
Human rights called
Freedom
Life
Liberty and
The pursuit of happiness
The programming persecutes your Spirit beliefs
Belittles your Spirit accomplishments
Makes your Spirit feel inferior ... worthless
The conformists will give you so-called help ... relief
Then cause you to feel ashamed or stupid
Because you asked for help
The programming dimensions are void of connection
A reason why you feel a void while
Immersed in the programming

The programming will put you off guard when your love and devotion to The Infinite Spirit is disconnected. The programming only needs a breath to sneak back into your life ... it is a thin line. You think you are praising The Infinite Spirit and wham! You recognize that you are praising human Spirits and all their statues and idols that have been created for you to worship and idolize.

Conformist programming
Rules in the Lower Dimensions of The Infinite Spirit
It consists of men and or women Spirits ruling other Spirits
Creating all the programming dimensions of madness
Their main programming tool is
Money and power
They do not think about happiness, friendship or love
They are cold, calculating and backstabbers
They are rude, hateful and destructive
They talk words of business only
They want only things of a material nature
Other human Spirits are insignificant
If they do not think ... if they do not act
In the same manner

The programming resides in dimensions of
The corporate structure

Resides in money
Lies ... hard labor
Prejudice, hate and slavery
Resides in games
Stress ... sorrow
Resides in fantasylands
Illusions ... delusions
Resides in madness
Experimentation ... death
All which break your Spirit and
Promote eventual death of
Your physical body
Before it is time

The human Spirit is set up for failure in this programming where conformist law is, 'what I say, you must obey ... obey ... obey'! It does not matter what your Spirit tells you. You are programmed to see yourself as a sinner, lowly and not worthy of being in the presence of The Infinite Spirit. You are set up to keep your powerful Spirit imprisoned by the programming madness and ignorant to "What's Really Going On".

The programming teaches a craving
For an existence initiated for manipulation
To worship money while
Thou shalt have
No graven images
Before thee

Money is one of the primary temptations of the programming which keeps you playing the never-ending dimensions of games which immerse you in a life of madness. The programming works for those who are dependent upon money for their survival and living as opposed to being independent in the knowledge that you are a Child of The Infinite Spirit and therefore, will survive under any circumstances. Daily the conformists scheme to keep the trends changing and the game strategies updated. They strive to retain their power over other human Spirits. Human Spirits are the game pieces that they strategize with. Human Spirits are caught in dreams for supremacy while being taken away from their Spirit connection to The Infinite Spirit.

The programming dimensions of money bring out the worst in a Spirit
Money promotes programming dimensions
Of hate

Prejudice
Greed
Money makes slaves of
Men, women and child Spirits
For the purpose to mass produce
Mo' money, mo' money and mo' money
All Spirits have become slaves
They call you managers, supervisors, workers
They call you Black, Brown, Red, Yellow and White
Workers who put
Mega money in the pockets of
Corporations and politicians
Workers who work hard for the money
Only to give it back to
The corporations and politicians who
Appeal to the programmed child
Corporations which advertise their products to
Be essential for you
To live happily ever after

"Come on down! We want you to buy all these things to make your
house look nice"!

Is this not an insult? How are you going to imply that my house does
not look nice unless I buy your products? I do not think so!

Oh yeah! I hear you …
You do not have to buy them.
But, you usually do, huh?
Because you have been programmed to
Buy, buy and buy some more
And you go into debt
Trying to have a house with expensive material things
Things that could be gone
In the blink of an eye
You want to wear clothes that are in fashion
And that fashion season
Changes four times a year
You must have a new car every year
Trying to out-do
Trying to look beautiful
When you are beautiful to begin with

Trying to be a clone
Accepting insults left and right
Disrespect everywhere
Spending money you do not make enough of
Money you do not have
Making your struggle deeper and deeper
Avoiding the reality that
You are programmed to
Bring this struggle on yourself
By buying into the fantasies
You accept the programming of
Humiliation
Anguish
Imprisonment
You have bought into
Desiring
The programming dimensions of madness

Recognize that you are deep in it ... money deep in it! Recognize that you are the men, women and children being bought and sold. Recognize that you are the slaves no matter what race, creed or color. The only escape from the madness is to recognize that you are living in the programming dimensions of madness. Yes! It is difficult to escape because you have been programmed to live only with this programming in the lower dimensions and to love the challenges of surviving the demands, stress and pressure.

Know that these conformists are also of The Infinite Spirit and that these are the dimensions they choose and force you to choose. Yours is not to judge but to recognize. Whatever ... it is all of The Infinite Spirit!

Today, April 24, 2006, Oprah's show was about a three year old female child who gets upset about not looking beautiful and cries to put make-up and fingernail polish on. There was also a four year old female child who thinks that she does not look good unless she is skinny. Dr. Robin Smith said that we mothers are passing on our insecurities to our daughters through the birth canal. I agree.

I also say that these insecurities, habits, etc. that we acquired from our mothers are programming dimensions of insecurities. These children today are expressing those programming dimensions of their mothers and fathers and their mothers and fathers, etc., etc., etc.

When I was born in 1945, there was no awareness or acknowledgement of that passing of low Spirit esteem. Now, in 2006, that low or no Spirit esteem is still affecting our children's Spirits and the programming is ingrained in their aware thinking at earlier ages. This programming is taking Spirits to a level of no return without a chance of "Ultimate Respect" being implemented. "You Better Recognize"! Awaken to "What's Really Going On"!

One of the objects of the programming is to overshadow and annihilate your Spirit connection to The Infinite Spirit. You are led to believe that you have to suffer unbearable pain for the so called sin you commit. Conformist Spirits say they forgive you but, in the programming dimensions, they are only words because you are reminded of your sins for as long as you allow yourself to take on a guilt attitude.

The programming rules cover all angles. There is a game for every attitude, every thought, every action and reaction. All is answered logically. Look up the meanings for logic. You will see that logic is of conformist ideology. There are many books for your reference on the theories of logic. Their answers overpower instinctive and balanced thinking. Your Spirit energy is suppressed.

Know that The Infinite Spirit inflicts a consequence so that you will strengthen your Spirit to prepare you for exploring and experiencing in the Upper Dimensions of The Infinite Spirit. Know that the suffering does not have to be so devastating that the pain inflicted is more than intended. The Infinite Spirit wants you to learn. The conformists act higher than The Infinite Spirit and judge The Infinite Spirit as too easy going … a pushover. The conformists programming has laws conflicting with The Infinite Spirit's Laws and stretches them to satisfy their mentally unbalanced programming, which pampers their guilt feelings and gives justification to their narrow-mindedness and their need to feel powerful.

Human Spirits are sinners
Because they do not see themselves connected to The Infinite Spirit
Human Spirits are sinners
Because the programming programs you to see yourself as a sinner
This programming introduces you to guilt
Guilt pulls you deeper into this programming which
Captivates
Your feelings, thoughts, actions and being
This guilt hinders you from taking chances
And you embark on an endless search

For a happy and peaceful life
You see no chance to take a chance
To have a better life
Know that
In this programming, confusion is injected
Fears are instilled
Hurt is inflicted
And love of human Spirits is abandoned
You no longer have to explore and experience dimensions of abuse
Dimensions of disrespect
You no longer have to lie to protect yourself
Reconnect your Spirit to The Infinite Spirit
Your Spirit who deserves love
Your Spirit worthy of "Ultimate Respect"
"Reconnect"!

When you awaken your Spirit, you will be able to release the programming which keeps you in prison!

How much are you familiar with the programming dimensions?

The programming dimensions promote
Seeing love as pain
Getting angry at the people you love
Prejudice against any and, eventually, all things
Waking up to an alarm clock every morning, afternoon or evening
Working eight or more hours a day ... five days a week
They are now trying to program Spirits
To work 12 or more hours a day and six days a week
Giving less time for self

Programming is saying you did not when you did
Saying you did when you did not
Doing what you are taught to do
Saying what you are taught to say
Thinking how you are taught to think ONLY
Believing the lies
Believing and swearing by the programming dimensions ONLY!

The programming is one perspective in control breeding disrespect, disrespect and more disrespect!

The programming strives to enslave every Spirit on planet Earth and that includes animals and plants. I was watching the History Channel and listening to Eastern Philosophy when a picture came on showing a man steering a plow that oxen were pulling. I felt the Spirits of those oxen. My eyes saw their enslavement. I then thought of slaves in the cotton fields with the ultra hot sun beating on their Spirits with their every step exerting vital energy needed for survival. I felt those oxen trying to hurry the day so that they could rest.

I said that to say this: enslavement is a prerequisite item of the programming. Know that while you are immersed in the programming, you will be enslaved, tired and rushing the moments; not to live each moment to the maximum but, to hurry up and get the moments over. Are you appreciating and living the moments or rushing them away?

Have you awakened? Do you see how the programming dimensions will cause you to subliminally look at your Spirit with disgust? Your constant exploring and experiencing in these programming dimensions enable your physical body to push your Spirit awareness into hibernation. You are out of focus and unable to recognize, hear or think of other Dimensions of The Infinite Spirit. Your physical body and your Spirit settle into complacency as you grow fast into programming comfort. You ache with every breath. You are confused, continuously mesmerized and blind to the programming dimensions.

Wake Up Call! It's A Wake Up Call Y'all!

CHAPTER NINE

KNOW THE WORD!

Mature

Through recognition of the word

The programming

Reflects

Dual purpose

Through the word

Giving creation

To a

Multi-faceted

Word

Everything has its own particular dimension which sustains it ... which makes it what it is ... which gives it life or death. The letters of words each have their own dimensions of purpose and programming dimensions of purpose. I suggest that you start examining words, for their letters have living energy. You are connected or controlled through the word. Become aware of hidden programming dimensions. Recognize what you are reading at all times. The programming concentrates on specific definitions which will hold your thoughts in a state of tunnel vision causing you to continually explore and experience through programming dimensions.

Have one or more dictionaries within reach. Definitions clarify! When you look for the definition, be sure to read and know every definition of every word in the definition. Definitions change from year to year as past definitions are deleted and replaced with new definitions which purport control.

I only include a few words that were enlightening to me, in one form or another. It is up to you to examine other words. The following definitions are from "The American College Dictionary, 1947" or, "Webster's New World Dictionary, Second College Edition, 1976", or "Webster's Desk Dictionary of the English Language 1983", or "The Oxford Universal Dictionary on Historical Principles, Third Edition 1944".

Natural
Of or arising from nature
In accordance with what is found or expected in nature
Of the real or physical world as distinguished from a spiritual,
intellectual, or imaginary world
Without legal relationship, specifically illegitimate (a natural child)
A person without normal intelligence
A fool
An idiot

These definitions were most interesting. What do you make of the third definition? Of course, legal and normal refers to conformist programming. Think of all the guilt perpetuated by illegitimate. I once thought of fool and idiot as negative words, and then I thought about most of the folks they threw into insane asylums and they called them fools. I will bet they were not insane. They probably were connected to The Infinite Spirit but, the knowledge they were spouting was not of the <u>normal</u> persuasion and not what the conformists wanted other Spirits to hear and or think about. How do you suppress knowledge you do not want revealed? You cut off their heads--not physically; but mentally and spiritually.

Illegitimate
Not recognized as lawful off springs, specifically, born of parents not
married to each other
Departing from the regular
Not sanctioned by law
Illegal

The words of interest here are lawful, regular and not sanctioned by law … meaning conformists' programming laws.

Fool
A person lacking judgment or prudence
One who is victimized or made to appear foolish
Dupe
A harmlessly deranged person
One lacking in common powers or understanding

Foolish
Marked by a loss of composure

Judgment, victimized, dupe, common, loss of composure. All of these words relate to what is expected of an upstanding conformist character. If you rebel against that expectation, you are labeled a fool or foolish; and, who listens to a fool?

Awe
Dread
Terror
The <u>power to inspire</u> dread
Profound and reverent fear inspired by deity
Abashed fear <u>inspired by authority or power</u>
<u>To control or</u> <u>check by inspiring with awe</u>

Dread
To fear greatly
Great fear, esp. of impending evil
Reverential fear
Awe
An object of fear or awe
Exciting great fear
Dreaded
Inspiring with awe
Venerable

Terror
State or instance of extreme fear
Violent dread
Fright
Terribleness
A person or thing that causes extreme fear
One difficult to manage
A great nuisance
A state of <u>intense fear caused by the systematic use of violent means by a party or faction to maintain itself in power</u>

Fear
Profound reverence and awe, especially toward God
Frighten
To feel fear in oneself
To have a reverential awe of (fear God)
To be afraid of
<u>Fear implies anxiety and usually loss of courage</u>
Fearful applies to <u>what produces</u> fear, <u>agitation</u>, or <u>loss of courage</u>
Awful implies <u>striking with</u> <u>an over-powering awareness</u> of transcendent
force, might or significance
Terrific implies the <u>power to stun or strike terror</u> with the release or
display of great explosive force
Afraid may or may not imply good ground, but usually <u>suggests
weakness or cowardice</u>

Awful
Inspiring awe
Filled with awe
Terrified
Afraid
Deeply respectful or reverential

Are these the words you want lurking around your Spirit?

Reverence
Suggests a <u>self-denying acknowledging</u> of what has an intrinsic and
inviolate claim to respect

*We are told to fear God (whose name refers to man ... have you looked
up the definition for god?) ... in awe ... in reverence. All that fear, terror
and self-denial is being reflected to your Spirit who obeys The Word of God.
When you fear something, you tend to back away from it, hide it and deny
it. No wonder folks find it difficult to respect their Spirit! Look at the fear
... the terror ...the self-denial you hold in your Spirit when you buy into the
program of fearing God.*

god
A being of more than attributes and powers
A deity, <u>esp. a male deity</u>
<u>Anything worshipped by man as a deity</u>
<u>An idol</u>

God
<u>The Supreme Being</u>
The eternal and infinite Spirit
Spirit
Sovereign of the universe
<u>The ruler or sovereign embodiment</u> of some aspect
Attribute of reality as the god of love
A supreme being <u>conceived as a world soul</u>; as the pantheistic god
<u>A person or thing defiled</u>

God *Christian Science*
Incorporeal
Divine
Supreme
Infinite Mind
Spirit
Soul
Principal
Life
Truth
Love - *Mary Baker Eddy*
To treat as a god; to deify

The first thing that came to my Spirit was the order of the definitions with little g as the first series of definitions. And then, wow! Male deity, supreme being, idol, ruler, person defiled ...? Sounds like conformist programming! "What's Really Going On"?

Sovereign
Chief or highest
Supreme
Supreme in power
Superior in position to all others, specifically, princely and or royal
Independent of, and unlimited by any other
Possessing, or entitled to, original and independent authority or
jurisdiction; as, a sovereign state.
Efficacious
Effectual, as a remedy
Synonym - see dominant
<u>A person, body of men, or state, vested with sovereign authority</u>

Sovereignty
Quality or state of being sovereign
The status, dominion, or rule of a sovereign
<u>Supreme political power or authority</u>

(A definition of God is sovereign of the universe!)

Instinct
A <u>natural or inherent</u> aptitude, impulse or capacity
A largely inheritable and unalterable tendency by an organism to make
a complex and specific response to environmental stimuli without
involving reason

Reason -- of conformists' programming.

Instinctive
Prompted by natural instinct or propensity
Arising spontaneously and <u>being independent of judgment or will</u>

Moral
Expressing or teaching a <u>conception of right behavior</u>
Conforming to the standard of <u>right behavior</u>
Probable though <u>not proved</u>
Of, relating to or acting on the mind, character or will

Morality
A doctrine or <u>system</u> of moral conduct
Conformity to ideals of right human conduct

Right behavior by whose standards? Conformist programming ideology.

Normal
According with constituting, or <u>not deviating from a norm, rule, of
principle</u>
Regular
Of, relating to, or characterized by <u>average intelligence or development</u>

Normalize
<u>To make conform</u> to or reduce to a norm or standard

Think
To form or have in the mind
To have as an option
Believe
<u>To devise</u> by thinking
To form an idea or think <u>implies the entrance of an idea into one's mind
with or without deliberate consideration or reflection</u>

The important word here is to devise. Devise means to create. When you think, your Spirit creates what your aware thoughts are thinking.

Gravitate
To move or tend to move under the influence of gravitational force
<u>To tend toward the lowest level</u>
<u>Sink</u>
<u>Fall</u>

Your physical body is programmed to gravitate to the lowest ebb in the Lower Dimensions of The Infinite Spirit.

Experience
The observing, encountering, or undergoing of things generally as they occur in the course of time
Knowledge of practical wisdom gained from what one has observed, encountered, undergone

Your whole life is one experience after another. Release your programming experiences.

Friend
A person whom one knows well and is fond of
Intimate associate, close acquaintance
A person on the same side in a struggle
<u>One who is not the enemy or foe</u>
Ally

To be a friend is not only to others, but most importantly, to your Spirit.

Love: [1947]
A feeling of strong personal attachment induced by sympathetic understanding, or by ties of kinship
Ardent affection

69

The benevolence attributed to <u>God as being like a father's affection for his children</u>
<u>Men's adoration of God</u>
Strong liking
Fondness
Good will
Tender and <u>passionate</u> affection for one of the opposite sex
The object of affection
Sweetheart
Cupid, or Eros, as god of love
Sometimes, Venus
Tennis, nothing; no points scored - used in counting the score

[1976]
A deep and tender feeling of affection for or <u>attachment</u> or devotion to a person or persons
A feeling of brotherhood and good will toward other people

[1983]
A profoundly tender, <u>passionate</u> affection
A feeling of warm personal attachment
<u>Sexual desire</u> or its gratification
A beloved person
A strong predilection or liking for something
Tennis. A score of zero
In love (with)
Feeling deep, affection or <u>passion</u> (for)
Make love
To woo or court
To embrace and kiss
<u>To engage in sexual intercourse</u>
To have love or affection (for)
To have a strong liking (for)

Are these your definitions of love? Man's adoration of God? Remember one definition of God is male deity. Sounds like programming dimensions of love. "What's Really Going On"? These are not the definitions of love in the Upper Dimensions of The Infinite Spirit!

Passion: [1947]

<u>THE ENDURING OF INFLICTED PAIN, TORTURES, OR THE LIKE</u>

The <u>suffering</u> of Christ on the cross, or his <u>sufferings</u> between the night of the Last Supper and his death

The <u>sufferings of a martyr</u>

Martyrdom

One of the gospel narratives of the passion of Christ

State or being <u>affected by external agents or forces</u>

Feeling

Emotion; specif., one of the <u>feelings natural to all men, as fear, hate,</u> love, joy; pl., these emotions collectively

<u>Violent or intense emotion; emotional excitement or agitation</u>

<u>Rage</u>

<u>Wrath</u>

Ardent affection for one of the opposite sex

Love

Sexual desire

<u>Lust</u>

An object of love, deep interest, or zeal

[1983]

Any powerful emotion or feeling as love or <u>hate</u>

Strong affection

Strong sexual desire

A strong fondness or enthusiasm

The object of such a fondness

An outburst of strong emotion or feeling

The sufferings of Christ on the cross or His sufferings subsequent to the Last Supper

Stop your desires to have passion! Passion means suffering. Stop your desires to suffer! Your calling for passion brings you suffering. What programming illusions are you asking to come into your relationships? Recognize that if you desire passion, you call for suffering ... inflicted pain ... torture ... rage to enter your life!

Suffer: [1933]

To undergo

Endure

To have <u>something painful, distressing</u>, or injurious inflicted or impose upon one

To <u>submit to with pain, distress, or grief</u>

71

To go or pass through
To be <u>subjected to pain, punishment, or death</u>
To <u>tolerate, allow</u>
To bear with
Put up with
To allow oneself to <u>submit to be treated in a certain way</u>
Consent to do or be something

[1945]
To submit to or be forced to endure
Bear as a victim or patient
To undergo; experience; pass through
To have power to resist or sustain
To <u>undergo pain of body or mind</u>
Archaic To endure or tolerate an evil
Injury

Hmmmmm! Better really rethink your quest for passion.

Recognize
To <u>know again</u>
To perceive to be a person or thing previously known
To <u>avow knowledge of</u>; to admit with a formal acknowledgment
To acknowledge formally as by special attention
To take notice of
To acknowledge with a show of approval; as, to recognize services
To acknowledge acquaintance with, as by salutation

Armageddon
The place of great battle to be fought on "the great day of God" <u>between the powers of good and evil</u>
Any great final conflict

Wake Up Call! It's A Wake Up Call Y'all!

CHAPTER TEN

YOU ARE A BEAUTIFUL SPIRIT

My interpretation of Spirit respect goes deep. It goes to the very core of my energy. Do not take it lightly when I say that you must like, accept, love and respect you. Recognize when your physical body is in a programmed mode. Let it know that you are not going that route any longer.

Know you ... all of you! This is the most important thing that needs to happen in your life at this moment! You deserve "Ultimate Respect"!

Know you so that you will make the right choices for you. Some of the choices I made for me may not be the right choices for you but, it is possible that they will lead you to the right choices for you. You always have a choice! Choose wisely!

Bring you to new dimensions of aware thoughts. These new dimensions will bring different laws ... different truths. Release those programming thoughts and habits which cause you to continually explore and experience programming dimensions of hurt, anger and depression which affect you, other Spirits you love and other Spirits around you.

You have the power to be a winner in everything that is beneficially desired when your Spirit is followed. Stay in tune with your Spirit. Know your Spirit so completely that it becomes automatic to follow your Spirit connection to The Infinite Spirit without a second thought.

Recognition brings answers to questions that seem impossible to answer. For example, why are people so cold, mean and or hateful? How do they do some of the horrible things they do? Recognize that their thoughts and actions are deep into the programming as yours were and or are.

Recognize
That The Infinite Spirit gives guidance
The Infinite Spirit gives direction
To guide you through the dangers
To guide you through the programming that is invading your aware thoughts
That is invading your physical body
That is invading your Spirit

Recognize your ignorance
Of disrespecting your Spirit
Find the "Ultimate Respect" that you deserve

Recognize the programming dimensions which haunt your Spirit
You were not meant to go through such trials

Make the right choices
Release the dimensions of programming madness

Recognize that examining "What's Really Going On"
Brings a problem to a solution

Recognizing is listening to everything and
Having those areas clarified that are questionable

"You Better Recognize"!

To like, accept, love and respect you is not a selfish act or thought when it remains in a balanced manner. To like, accept, love and respect you is the greatest gift you will give to your Spirit and other Spirits. To like, accept, love and respect you is reconnecting one of the Infinite Spirit's Children!

You say you been sleeping, sleeping and sleeping
And just want mo' sleep, mo' sleep and mo' sleep
You have no ambition to get up out of the bed
Listen to me … you are depressed!
The programming has your Spirit in dimensions of
Hiding deep within your physical body
Get out of the bed
Awaken your Spirit from hibernation
It is time to get out the funk
Shed that programming … you don't need that junk
I'm telling ya … release that programming junk
Plain and simple … get out the funk!

Wake up your Spirit
Make the right choices for your Spirit
Let right now be the first moment of the rest of your life
Change what's around you
Put sunshine into your life
Open your curtains … let the sun touch your skin
Absorb the sun's wonderful energy
The Infinite Spirit put it there for you
Re-energize … re-energize
Wake the funk up!

You're alive ... be alive!
Get out the funk!
Take a walk ... breathe in some fresh air
Talk to a tree and that tree will give you energy ... try it and see
Give a greeting to everyone ...
Smile!
Make someone else's day
Hug your mother ... your father
Your Sista ... your brutha
Your daughter ... your son
Hug them tight!
Oh yeah ... they may think you are crazy

There's nothing wrong with crazy ... get crazy!
Do something crazy like live!
Live my friend! Live!
Get excited about your life!

Stop your confessing
Give up your depressing
Change! You are not insane!
Don't sabotage your Spirit again
Change all that programming madness you are in
And, it ain't about smoking or drinking that wine or that gin

It is about caring for your Spirit
It is about becoming your best friend
It is about lifting your Spirit
Awakening your Spirit from hibernation
It is about cleansing the toxins from your physical body
The programming has you in a funk
Release
Release
Release all of that maddening junk
Get out of that funk!

Wake Up! Wake Up! Wake Up!

YOU MUST GET SERIOUS

Reach deep within the bowels of your Spirit and
Extract the Child of The Infinite Spirit
Recognize your Spirit

Blossom Child of The Infinite Spirit!

Always be pleasant giving forth balanced energy. We help others by giving out balanced energy. It is like you fortifying their deeply suppressed unbalanced energy. You give them a boost so that they can restore the balance in their life which in turn fortifies your Spirit.

Develop patience which is one of many important factors that will assist you in getting your Spirit together. You will have many dimensions of programming habits which will come to your awareness that will have to be released. Face them. You set the terms. Live your life for the benefit of you first. You are here to see the beauty of your precious Spirit at all times. You are here to reconnect therefore, you must strive to continuously like your Spirit, accept your Spirit, love your Spirit and respect your Spirit! Only "Ultimate Respect" for your Spirit!

Recognize that the depths of liking, accepting, loving and respecting your Spirit must be deep in order for you to explore and experience the Upper Dimensions of The Infinite Spirit. It will take time. How much time depends upon how much you want to live through your Spirit. Recognizing "What's Really Going On" will become easier with each stronghold you crumble. Your strength magnifies when your goal is to awaken your Spirit, awaken your Christ Dimension within your Spirit, give your Spirit "Ultimate Respect" and reconnect with The Infinite Spirit!

It is those programming dimensions surrounding you
Those programming dimensions you grew up with that
You have to break through
See you busting through those programming dimensions
Then, feel you smile!

Think about your thoughts and actions
Before you send them out to affect someone else
Know which thoughts will bring happiness and peace
Know which thoughts will bring pain and turmoil
Think before you send them out
Send them with the utmost care

Remember that your concentration goes to recognizing and respecting your Spirit and with that respect, your physical body will also be respected; for without your physical body, your Spirit will not learn what needs to be learned in these lower dimensions.

More and more people are getting caught in their programmed sinful ways. Money, crime, sex, children, cigarettes, alcohol and drugs are the primary targets. These are the major things which distract the Spirit from knowing what's really going on. People are lying, stealing, murdering and tainting their innocence for the love of money. They try to find happiness and the crimes go on and on.

People are controlled by their physical bodies as they try to find happiness through their fantasies with other physical bodies. Their targets are wild pornography, wild toys and children. What have we allowed to happen to the children?

People, especially the youths are mesmerized by the alcohol and drugs as they try to find happiness through the momentary freeing of the Spirit. This momentary freedom may end with anger, dementia, tormenting fears and sometimes death of the physical body which ends the Spirit's explorations and experiences before it is time to end.

It is time for parents to step up and teach their children what they need to know! Children must be taught about who they are first and foremost. Children must be taught about the programming at birth because the programming starts its hard-core programming at birth. Let them know the consequences of choosing to be controlled by money, crime, sex, alcohol and drugs ... let them know how they slowly kill the physical body. Your children need your love, guidance and truth about what's really going on! Material love is no substitute for Spirit love!

YOU ARE MOST IMPORTANT
Every nook and cranny of you
Protect you
Give you
Your family
Your friends
Other Spirits
"Ultimate Respect"
Your children are learning the most from you
If you want them to be responsible
You must be responsible

What you want from other Spirits
You must demand from you first
Be honest with you and other Spirits
Be faithful to you
Stick to your commitments to you
Tell the truth
Practice what you preach

It is time to awaken you-your Spirit? It is time to make the commitment to you. Yes! It is scary because you do not want to make any mistakes this time. But this time, you will be able to correct the mistakes quickly. It is scary because you see this time as no turning back to what you once thought was the only life you would ever have. No turning back to the programmed you.

Wake Up Call! It's A Wake Up Call Y'all!

CHAPTER ELEVEN

THE LOVE YOUR SPIRIT DESIRES

THE LOVE YOUR SPIRIT DESIRES IS IN THE UPPER DIMENSIONS OF THE INFINITE SPIRIT WHICH ARE DIMENSIONS OF "ULTIMATE RESPECT"!

What is love? There are many dimensions of love. There is programming love, parental love, child love, sister love, brother love, friend love, spousal love, and ultimate respect love for all that is of The Infinite Spirit. Love may be friendship where a Spirit is truthful, respectful and acknowledges The Infinite Spirit first. This is love in The Infinite Spirit's Upper Dimensions. Love can be hate where a person loves the hate she or he harbors. This is programming love in The Infinite Spirit's Lower Dimensions. What dimension is your love residing in?

The problem with love nowadays is that it is explored and experienced in the programming dimensions. It is sad to see that in the programming, the meaning of friendship changes. The honesty, the trust and the love change to programming dimensions of games promoting programming dimensions of hurt, anger, hate and death. Human Spirits miss out on exploring and experiencing dimensions of beautiful love. Unconditional love becomes lost to dimensions of conformist love.

The programming dimensions of love promote Spirit disrespect. This type of love is the only love that is known and conflicts prevail. You think you like, accept, love and respect you but, you do not. You want a lasting, happy and meaningful relationship but, you do not get it because you do not get exactly what you want from the programming dimensions of love. Many Spirits I have talked with think that you must have pain to experience true love. The dimensions of pain consist of programming techniques which cause your Spirit to ache in the illusion of pain. Love is no pain.

Women and men Spirits operate in different programming dimensions with men refusing to acknowledge the equality of women and women accepting their refusal. So our children become lost in programming dimensions of confusion, rebellion and perpetual ignorance. What are we allowing to happen to The Infinite Spirit's Children?

Women are learning about Spirit love
Of the Upper Dimensions of The Infinite Spirit
Women are teaching their daughters
Women are teaching their sons
About the respect they must have for their Spirit

They teach upper dimension love first and foremost
Mothers are letting their children know that
They are the teachers
They are the leaders of the future
Who will have to ensure
Continued balanced love and peace for planet Earth
And her seeds she gives life to

Women are learning to play business games
Just as men do
But these women are having problems with men
Because most men operate strictly in the programming and
Refuse to accept the changes
Refuse to give up their programming sense of power
Signifying that a 'real man' has
Muscles
Uncontrollable sex urges
Disrespect and
Hatred for women who want to be equal
Men do not want women playing
Their programming games
Because they would not be able to play war games
With their sons and daughters
Women need to pray that
Men awaken their Spirit from hibernation

He is a man who never learned how to love a woman
He just learned the exercises of the Kama Sutra
After which he went to sleep
He never learned how to love
Moms didn't show him
She was too busy holding down two jobs
Taking care of the other children
Taking care of the house
She was just plain worn out

Dads didn't know how to show him how to love
Being the bread winner symbolized
A man and his so called 'macho' nature
And macho was about manipulation
His was a programming of lord and master

He thought he was the king
But, he was in a program
Wake up ... wash up
Get dressed ... eat breakfast
Go to work for 8 to 16 or more hours ... come home
Take all the programming energy that you absorbed while
You were out of the house and
Lash out at those you love ...
Eat dinner ... watch TV
Go to bed after the eleven o'clock news
Then wake up and
Start it all over again

He never learned how to love a woman
He never learned how to feel the wonderfulness of a movement
He was a rhythm always out of sync
He never learned how to love a woman
He lost the natural instinct to love

Wake up call! It's a wake up call y'all!

Bring it back ... bring it back ... bring it back!

Think about the beautiful relationship two Spirits could have with each other using their own energy to their fullest capacity. Think about the disappointments that would be alleviated. Think about your dreams that would come true. It would be wonderful! A relationship with "Ultimate Respect"!

Know that it will be difficult to keep love in focus because in the programming dimensions, unbalanced energy surrounds you like a virus ... a seemingly incurable virus. Strive to guide your Spirit concentration to upper dimension love and respect.

I am Love
Do you know my wonderful dimensions?
No, I didn't think so because
My wonderful dimensions are
No pain ... no hurt
If you are exploring and experiencing
Dimensions of pain with me
If you are arguing with me
Abusing me

Lying to me
Cheating on me
Then you do not know
My wonderful dimensions
Because a balanced me is no pain … no hurt
Imagine that!

I, Love, am no pain!

Okay … so
Let's talk about the wonderful dimensions of me
Now wait a minute, do not get all funky!

Tell me what is the matter?
Was your love a victim of shatter?

Recognize and hear what I am saying
With your Spirit you must not be playing!

You see, I am dimensions of deep involvement … special joy
Wonderful happiness, no games … I am not a toy!

There is no death and misery surrounding and knocking at my door
It messes with happiness and
You should not endure that any more!

I am Love of exciting dimensions!

I am total fulfillment … laughter in the midst of marvelous
I am drenched in the feeling that is greatly yours to feel
You can take anything society has to deal!

I am wonder in the midst of joy
You had fun with me as a girl and boy!

I am contentment in the midst of bliss … gee
You would be insane not to want me!

Yes! I am love … the Spirit of Creation
My dimensions are happiness and miles of elation!

I create me through the marvelous wonder of birth
I am the uplifting dimensions in the universe
And that includes our planet Earth!

I devour your problems to simplicity … put oomph in your motivation
I am excitement in your smile … energy in your conversation!

I am no thought, no anger and certainly no pain
I am the cleanliness ... the freshness of a hot summer's rain!

I am Love of magnificent dimensions!

I fortify your reason for living ... I am not hard to find
Use my dimensions as the foundation for your peace of mind!

I am my friends, heaven in the midst of me
Release that mask of sneeeeky?

My dimensions are
Amazing
Gratifying
Sensational
I am Love, The Soul Of Creation!
All of my dimensions
Carry no pain
Do you know me?

Wake Up Call! It's A Wake Up Call Y'all!

CHAPTER TWELVE

ENDING

So, here it is February 26, 2007 … my brother's birthday ...

"Happy Birthday Bro"!

I know that I finally have the last chapter before my book goes to print. I do believe that things happen for a reason and when a situation occurs, the first things that I ask are, "Why did this happen? What's the purpose of me being in this place"?

This was my process of recent awakenings. On January 12, 2007, I saw a picture of my book cover. Approving the cover is the last phase before my book goes to print and comes out for the world to see. The cover is beautiful and exactly portrays my words! Matt Abdon surely displayed his genius! You know that I was too excited! All Praises to The Infinite Spirit!

On January 17th, my computer hard drive told me that it was ready to fail. I immediately called my son Darnell and he said that he would call his friend at Staples and get back to me.

On January 19th, Steve at Staples took my computer. I felt kind of lost because how was I going to check my bank balance, my emails and how was I going to make changes to my book cover? On second thought, I could send the changes to my book cover by mail but, at that time, it did not seem efficient because it would not get there as fast. I had convinced myself that I had to have my computer to send it by email that gets there instantly. Silly me!

The programming gets you even though you rise above it. You will fall back into a programming dimension in a flash! The beauty of being aware of this is that it does not take me months or years to realize that I am once again operating in a programming mode.

Anyway, I got my computer back on January 23rd. Thank you Steve! I appreciate you and Staples! I had to put programs back on. The only disc I did not have was Microsoft Word. I would have to buy another one. I had to wait until February to get that program. I was also waiting for a disc from AT&T to get my internet going again. I am calmly stressing.

January 24th Mama gets sick and has to be rushed to the hospital. She had congestive heart failure and multiple heart attacks. She is 85 and very frail. The doctor indicated that we should call everyone to say their goodbyes. My daughter Michelle took a week off from her job and took the night shift. My other daughter, Deserie and I were taking the day shift. We felt the need for someone from the family to be there with Ma 24 hours each day. I must say that Ma made it through! She's a tough lady! All Praises to The Infinite Spirit!

On January 26th, I was walking to Deserie's house which is two doors away and I snagged upon a hole and broke my ankle. There are people who will help you. Three cars stopped and helped to get me up from the ground. One beautiful lady drove me to my daughter's house. I want to thank those people who helped me. I appreciate you very much. All Praises to The Infinite Spirit for you!

I limped into Deserie's house and she told me to take the van to go to the hospital because she was tired. I limped to the van thinking that I only had sprained my ankle and drove to the hospital. I had to limp a long way to get to Ma's room and by the time I got there, the pain was activating. Michelle said to me, "Mom! I'm taking you to the emergency room"! A nurse retrieved a wheelchair for me and down I went to find out that I had broken my ankle and severely bruised my knee that is still swollen in some places.

So, here I am wondering again, what is the purpose for all of this? Well, one purpose was a wake up call for my family to wake up to the fact that everyone has to help to take care of Mama, especially my brothers! Actually, they would all have to help me and Mama. I was in the deep lockdown … bare minimum movement.

On February 22nd, I just knew this cast was coming off! After my visit with the doctor, he said that my ankle was doing well but, the cast would have to stay on another month. Later on that evening after I got over my disappointment and pouting, I saw the purpose of me still being in this cast. My book was waiting for me to write these realizations. And, guess what? I may not have ever seen that I needed to change the structure of this book had these potholes not been put in my path. All Praises to The Infinite Spirit!

And people, this is it! If I get any other awakenings, I will put them in another book. Am I hearing yaaayyy? So you agree? All Praises to The Infinite Spirit!

And now Spirits of The Infinite Spirit …

"The Spoken Book"! Part Two

All Praises to The Infinite Spirit!
Jehovah Sharma!
The Infinite Spirit's Presence is here! Hallelujah!

The moment
You feel hurt, used, abused, anger and disrespected is
The moment you ask yourself
Why do I feel this whatever it is?
What is the purpose for this madness?
What is the lesson I must learn?

I have been telling everyone that
This is a wake up call!
Ya know, that includes me
Me to get my book cover finished so that my book goes to print
The opportunities are everywhere, especially from The Infinite Spirit
But,
You have to act!
You have to get your Spirit up!
You know your Spirit has been Rip Van Winkle for a long time
It is time to wake up!

Awaken from your hibernation!
Wake your Spirit up everyday
And then your physical body
In that order!

Your Spirit needs no sleep! Wake up!

What I realized is that I had revisited the programming dimensions of
how to be
Get your eight hours of sleep
Talk like we talk
Be who I want you to be!

Say what?! I must buy how many outfits ... how many pairs of shoes ...
pay how much for rent ... pay how much for a house ... a car?

No wonder y'all are broke
Living paycheck to paycheck
Robbing Peter to pay Paul!

In my younger days, they didn't even talk in the figures that are out there now. When I was going to school, having $100 was like winning a million dollars! $100 was seldom seen, especially by a child! One penny could get you two squirrel nuts or some other kind of candy. You could get a bunch of junk with a nickel … and a buffalo nickel at that! If we only knew how much that buffalo nickel was going to be worth, we wouldn't have gotten that junk with a buffalo nickel!

Having said that …

Tonight, I represent Freedom

Have you seen the public service announcement
'What if America wasn't America'?
Then, on the screen flashes freedom
Well, that's me … freedom!

Oh my, what have I become?
Bills, bills and more bills
Folks really know how to show you how to spend your money
Working eight or more hours a day
Five to six … sometimes seven days a week
52 … and, if there were another … 53 weeks a year

Am I still of the people … by the people and … for the people?

You are paying too heavily for me
You work … you come home
Then you don't want to be bothered because
The job has taken … or rather
You have given your job all of your best energy
No time for self … no time for family or friends … no time for The Infinite Spirit

It appears that I am there for some of you
But, for most of you,
I have become your struggle
Taking all your energy struggle
No vacations … no new clothes … very little food
Struggle … a trying to survive struggle

Making 30 or 35 thousand dollars a year isn't anything

Most people are only making 10 to 18 thousand dollars a year
Taxes keep going up ... everyone trying to get a piece of your pie
Landlords and businesses keep going up on prices
Gas prices are making Bush Oil, Chaney and EXXON the best
investments
The kicker is no one is doing anything to stop it!

　　You call me freedom?!

As you remain in low brackets
Struggling
While wealthy folks are making billions a year
Millions are barely mentioned anymore
I know you feel my invasion gnawing at you ... pressing you
How are you making it?
Do you owe your soul to the company store?

Have I become greed?
Greed wanting and taking all that I can get with no thought of your
needs?

Have I become greed ... desiring more than I need?

Have I become greed ... growing stronger ... hurting you?

Have I become greed ... the seed of hate?

I am freedom!
Do you like what I have become?
Do you need to let go of me?
Have I become your killer?

　　How many of you feel free in this land of the free ... in these lands of
fantasylands?

Mother goose ... Mother goose
Lend me your ear
Trapped by a spider
At the end of the year
Who dat you say
Has summoned your tray
Go back to sleep

While fireflies I keep
To make way
For a dark and eerie day
Of mourning
As the bombs come without warning
All Spirits taken off their course of natural
Guess you like being the collateral
For the wild ways and foolish decisions of money
Depressed … regressed … no effervesce … just bullshit and baloney
They do it to your face
Grace tie up your shoe lace
They do it to anyone … anyplace
Oh, how we suffer
No chance for a buffer
Give up … give up … give up the ship!
The war
Let it be over
You have killed enough of our sons and daughters on this trip!

Why is the National Reserves fighting in this war started by greedy wealthy folks who always want the so called peons to fight their battles for them? What are the full time personnel of the Army, Navy, Air Force and Marines being trained for? Who's guarding the Country? Who is this freedom for? Is it for the United States? Is it for Iraq … Iran … Afghanistan? What's really going on?

The way I see it is my freedom is for those greedy CEO's and pharmaceutical companies whose job is to get all of your money that takes your freedom!

Oh yeah! Monkey see … monkey do … monkey be programming!
Do you see your monkey see … monkey do … monkey be programming?

Disrespect! Are you allowing yourself to be disrespected?
Are you often tempted by material things?
Is money that which has your undivided attention?

Are you monkey see … monkey do … monkey be whatever they want you to be?

Who are you taking orders from
Your physical body or your Spirit
The programming dimensions of The Infinite Spirit or
The Upper Dimensions of The Infinite Spirit?

I give you much to think about. Till we meet again, ask yourself:

Am I monkey see ... monkey do ... monkey be whatever they want me to be?

All Praises to The Infinite Spirit!

Wake Up Call! It's A Wake Up Call Y'all!

Hi Kindred Spirits! Wow! Do y'all know that you are beautiful?
No?
You better recognize!

Here I am ... in this elevator that has given a
'That's it ... I'm a retired' moment
A 'help ... I can't get up' moment!
Thank The Infinite Spirit for the electricity not going out.

Okay!
What is the reason for me getting stuck in this senior funk smelling elevator?
You know what they say when you get into a tight spot, "You need Jesus" ...
well, you elevator, you need Pine Sol ... I already have Jesus.

All Praises to The Infinite Spirit! Jehovah Sharma! The Infinite Spirit's
Presence is here! Hallelujah!

You will hear me say All Praises to The Infinite Spirit many times. It is not
because I am trying to push any religion on you. I am not in favor of the
expression, 'religious freak' ... I do not want any part of that programming
madness. It is that I carry The Infinite Spirit with me wherever I go and
I do not mind acknowledging the source of all things! All Praises to The
Infinite Spirit!

So let's get back to this broken down elevator. I really do not want to be in
here any longer than necessary.

Why am I in here ... inert ... stopped from carrying out my purpose?
What's really going on?
In the wrong place at the wrong time?
Nah! Nothing just happens.
You hear me?
Nothing just happens!

The programming will inconvenience you with pot holes as Bishop T.D.
Jakes would say.

Bishop T.D. Jakes is a great human Spirit who knows he is a Child of The
Infinite Spirit. He is out of the church programming dimensions and helps
you to get out of the programming dimensions. Oh yes! The church is the
one of the greatest programming tools of confusion! Be assured that Bishop
Jakes is not of those programming tools!

There are many people who give their perspective and follow their purpose. They all show you a way to escape the programming madness.

"Still I Rise" by Maya Angelou comes to my thoughts. Oh yeah! I rise up out of these dimensions of madness! I rise to the truth! I rise to reconnect to The Infinite Spirit! All Praises my Infinite Spirit!

I rise! I rise to tell you about the programming ... how to recognize it. I show you how to recognize who you really are!

Now, how many of you are hiding behind or
Hiding inside a physical body that has taken control of you
That has taken control of your Spirit?
I'm guessing all of you because of the alcohol and drugs you take
Legal and illegal!
There's no judgment here
You choose what you want for your life!
I'm just passing out information
A 'did you know?' kind of thing

Did you know that
Alcohol and manufactured drugs were created to keep your Spirit hidden
Created for your physical body to keep control of your Spirit
Created to keep your physical body wanting these depressants
Created to make your Spirit think that it is crazy
You know, loony-toons
Created to enslave your genius
Created to keep your Spirit in the programming dimensions
Created to keep you unstable?

The programming is that which tells you that it is my way or the highway! You must follow my programming rules or you may find yourself in an alley dead somewhere after I throw you out to the wolves, anacondas and piranhas as Rafaela would say.

You know that's cold!

The programming is catch 22 like a 'mammy jammie' as Sam Sawyer used to say.

Do you know Sam Sawyer? Sam Sawyer is a renowned basketball player who played professionally and then played with The Harlem Globetrotters. Sam is a beautiful Black man.

Oh no! I hope he knows he's Black!
Just kidding ... he knew ... he knew!

Sam was crazy funny ... always put a smile on your face. He met his match though when he tried to mess with me in spades. He talked much junk! But, I'd come back at him ...

"Okay! You want to mess with me? Oh! Aw ... oh ... oh ... looks like ten for two hundred Boy"!

He'd jump up with his tall, lanky self and say,

"Who you calling boy? Where's my dogs? I need my dogs! Uh ... don't you tell my dogs"!

Then the laughs and another game as he smiled while trying to be serious. Now, I must be honest. He did whupp my butt once in awhile! Sam, the man who everyone loved! Where you at Sam? I miss you! I love you!

Anywaaay ...
You must know that you get into situations for a reason or reasons. Ask yourself, "What's really going on"?

Uh oh! I hear someone!

"What's that you say? Yeah! There's someone in here. Huh? Yeah! I'm okay"!

Well, that's my cue folks. We will have to finish my talk at another time. I have so much to tell you! Uh oh! We're moving! All Praises to The Infinite Spirit!

It was nice talking with you all! Till next time ... ask yourself,

"What's really going on?"

Wake Up Call! It's A Wake Up Call Y'all!

Waaasup my Sisters and Brothers ... my kindred Spirits?

Are you ready to do some thinking about what's really going on?

Good because you have to question, examine and evaluate everything you think about, learn and hear!

After the death of Malcolm X and then Dr. Martin Luther King, Jr., Black folks were once again doing hard-core wandering. Yeah! We are still wandering – and you know this wandering includes all Races ... all Spirits of The Infinite Spirit ... accepting leftovers ... accepting programming hand me downs.

So, you think you wanna be a big boy ...
You think you wanna be a big girl
You think you wanna be an adult
You want to work, work and work some more
You wanna make your own money
You wanna get tired and stressed out
Not enjoying other things of life

You wanna false independence because
It's real hard ya know!
You wanna pay bills for the rest of your life
Looking for someone to help you
But someone is paying and wandering just like you!
So you wanna be a wanna be?

Wake Up Call! It's A Wake Up Call Y'all!

Things are not the way they seem
You have to check out "What's Really Going On"
Before you wanna be!

Oh yeah!
You will be wandering
Wandering into more programming dimensions of madness
Drowning in the programming
Trying to get deeper and deeper into the programming by wanting
Mo' money, mo' money and mo' money
Traveling further and further away from your genius ... your purpose
Further away from you-your Spirit
Repeatedly exploring and experiencing programming dimensions of
Hate, hurt, anger, depression, deceit and lies

Despising every moment of it
Punishing yourself
Being lied to
There are so many lies in the programming dimensions
Everything is a lie except your innocence
Except you-your Spirit!

You are immersed in programming dimensions of lies under the guise of it is alright to tell little white lies ... hmmmm ... interesting words in that saying!
It is time to wake up ... reverse the curse!

Let me remind you that you-your Spirit has no gender ... no ethnic background. You are The Infinite Spirit's Child who is wandering in The Infinite Spirit's Programming Dimensions of hell in the Lower Dimensions of The Infinite Spirit.

You know what I say!

Wake up! Wake up! Wake up!

Step out of the programming dimensions of madness ... step out of hell!

So my kindred Spirits, I hope you are waking up to what's really going on! Until more awakenings the next time ... I love you all! All Praises to The Infinite Spirit!

Yo! How much do you wanna be a wanna be?

WAKE UP CALL! IT'S A WAKE UP CALL Y'ALL!

Hey my Sisters and Brothers ... and I now know that you are my sisters and brothers because we originate from the same Ultimate Source! Isn't that marvelous!

All Praises to The Infinite Spirit!

So you say you have no self-esteem?
Do you hate yourself?
Are you accepting disrespect everyday?
Are you deep in depression?
Do you want to die?
Are you feeling lost in fantasyland after fantasyland?
Are you caught in lie after lie?
The NBC series 'Passions' has great examples of programming dimensions of lies.

Do you think that you may be immersed in the programming dimensions of madness ... deep in its clutches?

Well, you know what I say,

Wake up! Wake up! Wake Up!

Wake you-your Spirit up!
Wake the you up who has been hibernating
The you that should be making the choices for your living
Wake the you up who has been overlooked ... cut down ... highly disrespected
The you who has been imprisoned by the programming dimensions
You must wake up to see what's really going on!
Wake up Spirit!
Take your control back!

You say you have no self-esteem?
Do you hate yourself?
Are you accepting disrespect everyday?
Have you ever thought about giving yourself "Ultimate Respect"?

Well, you know what I say,

Wake Up! Wake Up! Wake up!

Start demanding "Ultimate Respect"
From you and other Spirits!
You are a precious Spirit ... a Child of The Infinite Spirit!

Accept nothing less than "Ultimate Respect"!
Always give you "Ultimate Respect"!

A thought just popped into my head ...

You know, even if you are a so called alien from another planet, galaxy, space, etc., etc., etc., you still originated from The Infinite Spirit! Hallelujah! All Praises To The Infinite Spirit!

Please, take care of you! I love you my Sisters and Brothers! Till the next time we meet.

Accept only "Ultimate Respect"!

Wake Up Call! It's A Wake Up Call Y'all!

Good evening beautiful Spirits! Get relaxed and ride on my thoughts for you!

All Praises to The Infinite Spirit!
Jehovah Sharma!
The Infinite Spirit's Presence is here! Hallelujah!

Tonight, we are in a long line waiting to see a basketball game.

Look at all these people! I wonder how many of them know their Spirit? Tonight, I am with one of those Spirits deeply immersed in the programming dimensions of money and look at me ... ain't I fine?

Oh yeah! I said yes when he asked me to go with him!

The Infinite Spirit did not say that I am not allowed to enjoy myself with the things in the programming dimensions. Just remember who you are and do not become immersed in the lies! Ya know? I know what is out of bounds for my purpose. And, why not get in on the stimulating energy of the fans? Joy is found everywhere. Know that when you are immersed in the programming dimensions of madness, fulfilling joy seldom happens.

How many of you think that this will be one of the best times you will ever have?

Where is your life?

I know that you are not thinking about you-your Spirit! I know that you are leading with your physical body that is telling you ...

"This is my present to you!
Don't I treat you good once in awhile?
This day is to show you that things aren't that bad ... that you can have fun and reconnect with wonderful dimensions but ... only for a moment ... uh ... a tease worth!

This day at this game is for the times I took all the control and led you deeper into the programming dimensions of madness. I'm letting you have a little breather – as they say.

This day is to keep me in control.
I know you will be grateful for me letting you have this one day ...
Say thank you! No! Not to The Infinite Spirit!
Say thank you to me ... your programmed physical body!
I create what you think, say and do and
Make sure you remember ... people are not supposed to see you-your Spirit

You know you are disgusting and ugly!
This is why you have to stay hidden and
You better not act up!
If you do, I will take you to the lowest depths of the programming!
You will not see a beautiful day anytime soon!
Now, who's in charge"?

Yes! Your physical body has that kind of hold when you are immersed in the programming dimensions.

Your physical body will keep you-your Spirit in darkness
Take you to the dimensions of lies
Leading you to dimensions of hurt after hurt
Sorrow after sorrow
Rape after rape
Anger after anger
Depression after depression
Hate after hate!

The physical body is great in its own right … in its own purpose. But, guess what? You-your Spirit is also great! This is why it is so important to know who you are. You must take your rightful place as a Child of The Infinite Spirit! You must take your control back!

Did you know that depression travels in the lowest ebbs of the programming dimensions … that depression explores and experiences the dungeons of desperate and wish I had a better life?

Are you depressed?

Well, you know what I say …

Wake up! Wake up! Wake up!

My attention just went to this thought …

I am the Spirit named Ruth Isaacs … daughter of Ike Isaacs – a wonderful jazz bass player. I loved my Father so much and was so very proud of him. He was pressed hard to not lead with his genius by a programmed female Spirit who broke his gentle protruding Spirit down. He put his anger … his programming sorrows in cigarettes which became his self punishment. He thought they were relieving his troubles. Instead, those cigarettes he called friends were slowly killing his physical body … choking his Spirit. Emphysema claimed his physical body at an early age. I know his Spirit has to explore more lessons from the programming dimensions because he left his body without having "Ultimate Respect" for himself.

In order to get out of the programming dimensions, you must give your Spirit and your physical body "Ultimate Respect"! You feel me?

Are you living through your physical body?
Are you exploring and experiencing programming dimensions of madness?
Dimensions you call sane ... normal ... the only way it is
Dimensions of tunnel vision ... stuck in a rut ... on your last dollar?
Know that when you are in these dimensions
You curse you
You disrespect you-your precious Spirit and your physical body
Causing your physical body to die before it is time.

Alright! The line is moving! Let's play ball! Until we meet again ...

Take your control back, enjoy and give your physical body and your spirit "Ultimate Respect"!

Wake Up Call! It's A Wake Up Call Y'all!

Thank you ... thank you all! It is wonderful to be here with you!

All Praises to The Infinite Spirit!

Hey! Hey! Hey!
How y'all beautiful Spirits doing?
Oh yeah, I'm liking this mic ... rophone!
Before I get into the sperm
Can I take just a moment of your time
Cause I want you to always shine

I'm in my shower a few hours ago
Thinking about talking with you marvelous Spirits ... my family
I want you to know that time really goes by fast
3 years ago, I was healthy ... I could outlast
But something grabbed me hard and
Took me out ... just choked my throat

Please think ... think ... think
Before you excessively smoke those cigarettes, do drugs and take too
much drink
You must take care of your body
It's toxic out there
And no one cares about you ... they just don't care!

Drink in moderation if you must
Cause you don't need no DUI or any kind of bust
Ya got to like, accept, love and respect yourself
Before you become ashes on a shelf

If you're having problems, come see me ... Dr. Woo
I'll help you learn how to take care of you
Get you together and sing a wonderful song
Before you know it, you're 60 and maybe even gone

Take care of you Baby!
Cause I love you and want you to be around for a long time
Know that you deserve the best life has to give you

Okay! Tonight, I represent the Sperm
That's right I said the Sperm
Someone has to represent

The program has you men believing that sex is going to improve your life!
That illusion may last 2 to 3 seconds when you have that orgasm but,
No pill or cream is going to make you have orgasms 24/7.

What!
You better wake up!

Sex does not improve your life
It depletes your energy
Renders you weak ... snore ... snore ... snore

What?
You know you guys have to have your beauty sleep!

Now, I'm not saying to stop having sex!
I'm saying value your sperm!
Don't throw them here, there and everywhere like they are worthless
For you know, they are priceless

What?
They are you incarnate! You men carry The Infinite Spirit's Sperm ... the seed of human life!

So I ask you ...
Are you banging the life out of you?

Bang ... ten years
Bang, bang ... twenty years
Bang, bang, bang ... thirty years
Bang, bang, bang, bang, bang, bang, bang
Oh no! What's that stuff called ... Viagra?

Wake Up call! It's a Wake Up Call Y'all!

Your sperm ... your seeds are precious. How much life do you have to lose?

Bang, bang, bang, bang, bang, bang, bang, bang, bang ...
Uh oh!
You're shooting blanks!

And then you go back to your angry and miserable self! What's really going on?

How long does your happiness last? How long before the anger?

Oh yeah! Here I am Anger. I relate your disappointments … your hurt …
your feelings of, "How could you do this to me? How could you do this to
me who is of the same essence as you? How could you disrespect me like
this? I thought you loved me"!

Who set your time bomb today?
What are you so angry about?
Who disrespected you today?

I, anger feel that it is my duty to
Let you know what my potential dimensions are
I, anger will make you act irrationally
I, anger will take you to dimensions of
The ultimate disrespect

And then,
I, anger, turn you into a time bomb
Ready to go off at any moment
I'm going off … I'm going off … I'm going off!
Grrrrrrrrrrrrrrrrr!

Whose path am I in? Grrrrrrrrrrrrrrrrr!
Your child?
I'm going off … I'm going off … I'm going off!
Grrrrrrrrrrrrrrrrr!
Did I take you to putting your child in a coma?

Whose path am I in? Grrrrrrrrrrrrrrrrr!
The love of your life?
I'm going off … I'm going off … I'm going off!
Grrrrrrrrrrrrrrrrr!
Did I take you to shooting your wife … your husband … your
sweetheart?

Whose path am I in? Grrrrrrrrrrrrrrrrr!
Your mother and or your father?
I'm going off … I'm going off … I'm going off!
Grrrrrrrrrrrrrrrrr!
Did I encourage you to cut off their heads?

Whose path am I in? Grrrrrrrrrrrrrrrrr!
You?
I'm going off … I'm going off … I'm going off!

Grrrrrrrrrrrrrrrrr!
Did I make you just kill someone over a beer?
Time bomb! Damn! I made you go off!

I am anger! Whew!
I am your worst enemy!
I beget rage ... rage begets hurt
Hurt begets more of me
More of me begets hate ... hate settles in the marrow of your bones and
Begets depression
I am deadly to you and others around you
Physically ... mentally ... spiritually
I am anger ... your time bomb about to go off!

Who were the ones
Who are the ones you met in my dimensions?
Have you apologized to them?
Have you apologized to you?
Are you going to prison because of me?

Every time you feel me coming on or
I'm already there
Stop ... think ... put me in check!
Release me ... release me ... release me before I go off!
This anger is telling you to wake up!
Have you heard about the Eleventh Commandment ...
THOU SHALT NOT BE ANGRY?

Because what?
I am anger!
I am your worst enemy!
I beget rage ... rage begets hurt
Hurt begets more of me
More of me begets hate ... hate settles in the marrow of your bones and
Begets depression
I am anger
I am deadly to you and others around you
Physically ... mentally ... spiritually
I am anger ... your time bomb about to go off!
Do not let me destroy you!

Alright beautiful Spirits ... till we meet again ...

Check your anger!

Wake Up Call! It's A Wake Up Call Y'all!

Hey, hey everyone! What's your temperature tonight? You know its

All Praises To The Infinite Spirit!

So, what should we talk about tonight?

Bitch! Did I just hear someone say bitch?

Okay! Tonight I represent the women you call bitch!

Come on Women ...
Ladies, you need to be suspicious
When your man does not want to take you out
When they have to hurry and get with the "G's"
Yeah, get with the G's who may also be getting your whoopee's
Hey, hey, it's the down-low
Disrespect ... disrespect ... disrespect

Women! Do not let these men see you as a dog ... here bitch!
A pussy ... here kitty, kitty!
Do not allow it!

It is 11 o'clock
Ring, ring ... hi!

Hey, what you doing?

Nothing!

What did you do all day?

Nothing! What did you do?

Oh, I had fun ... I was with my cousin ... We had a great time!

How wonderful for you!

I'm going to get something to eat. What time are you going to bed? Can I come over?

Oh! You've gotten your laugh on all day and now you want the whipped cream? I don't think so! No! No! No!

Well, I'll call you when I get home ... you know you my bitch!

Bye! Click!

My Sistas! This is how we are viewed and treated
Togetherness is gone

Enjoyment with each other is gone
Respect is gone
Appreciation is gone
Love is gone and
The programming goes on and on!

Why does a woman always have to be a bitch?
Don't you hate that word?
A man's knowledge of what a woman is and what she represents
Is diminishing to total disrespect!
Women are not bitches
They don't wear dog collars with stitches
Don't you hate that anyone sees a woman as that ...
Especially another woman!
It's degrading ... there are no dog bones here for trading!
You need to stop and think
Before your head gets whacked with the kitchen sink! Ouch!

From a very early age
Boys learn to call and see a woman as bitch
Not caring what the mere thought of the word denotes
A female dog ... garbage ... someone to stimulate your programming madness
No human Spirit I know deserves that!

I have a question for you fathers ... you men
Are you teaching your sons a way that intimidates you and your character?
Think about the consequences of
Teaching boys ... of teaching your sons that all women are bitches!

If this type of knowledge is continually bestowed
Then, what type of happiness will your son find
If he looks upon all women as bitches
In a world where folks do not want to have anything to do with
A woman who is referred to as a bitch!
And, you wonder why
Your sons are becoming gay!

You know what I say,

Wake up! Wake up! Wake up!

So, you will never forget September 11th
You will never forget the day your child died in Iraq
You will never forget April 16, 2007 at Virginia Tech
Will you remember how it changed you?
Do you remember the day you went back to business as usual?
Ya' know?
How long before you went back to who you were before the crisis?
How long before you went back to your 'I don't care attitude'?
How long before you went back to your programming dimensions of madness?
How long before you went back to accepting disrespect?

What happened to 'things need to change'?

You know you have to wake up to find out what the repercussions are from this programming mentality!

For instance, what things are really going into your body?

Awaken your Spirit …ask questions!
Recognize all they are doing to planet Earth!
Recognize what they are doing to the seeds of Mother Earth!
Recognize what they are doing to your physical body!
Recognize what they are doing to animals!
Crossbreeding … cloning … cloning … cloning
And then, you are eating the flesh and the insides of these animals
Of fruits
Of vegetables
And you don't even know what was in that seed!

The seeds … the seeds!
Recognize that they are changing the molecular structure of the seeds
Recognize that they are making them into chemical things
And, these chemical things that they are putting into these seeds are
Very toxic to us
Deadly to us
Causing your body to explode!

Oh yes! We need to go back to growing our own food
Raising our own animals
Sanitizing things
Being clean!
Things are dirty

People are dirty
Viruses are flying all over the place!
We need to go back to the cleanliness!
People don't wash their houses anymore
They don't do spring cleaning anymore!

What's in the air?
What's in the water?
What is going into your body?

So, my kindred Spirits, till we meet again remember that

"Ultimate Respect" means recognizing everything that is going on!

Wake Up Call! It's A Wake Up Call Y'all!

YOUR SPIRIT "ULTIMATE RESPECT" WILL RECONNECT YOU TO THE INFINITE SPIRIT EVERY MOMENT

Now that you know about the programming dimensions and have graduated from the Lower Dimensions of The Infinite Spirit, you will be subject to the gravity of the programming dimensions. You will be subject to backsliding. You will be subject to years of backsliding as long as your Spirit resides in your physical body.

Remember that thin line!

After you get excited about new knowledge, you must even think about and examine that knowledge to discover hidden contradictions and lies. Review all the choices to choose from, examine carefully and make your choice. If it works out, then you have made a beneficial choice for your Spirit. If it does not work out, keep choosing until you make the choice that will benefit your Spirit.

Your Spirit is blessed with having a physical body, connecting with the brain[4] and being able to explore and experience all the dimensions of The Infinite Spirit! These are wonderful blessings! You are given the privilege to be aware of who your Spirit is before you start your journeys of moving onward.

Being on planet Earth is one dimension of many that your Spirit will travel. You never stop learning. There will always be new explorations and experiences that will bring your Spirit to new insight. It is quite remarkable, amazing and wonderful when you have released those programming strongholds in the Lower Dimensions of The Infinite Spirit! You must remember your purpose for being here on planet Earth. You each have your particular purpose for your Spirit. I hypothesize that the main purpose we all have is to know The Infinite Spirit and explore and experience the infinite dimensions of The Infinite Spirit. Choose to awaken your Spirit, so that you will awaken your Christ Dimension and reconnect with The Infinite Spirit.

When planet Earth dies ... changes to another form, your Spirit will just be a part of space moving onward exploring and experiencing other dimensions of The Infinite Spirit. You will blend into The Infinite Creation. A possible consequence that I see if you stay immersed in the programming dimensions is that your Spirit will be stuck in the lower

---

[4] The Mind, Richard M. Restak, M.D.

dimensions promoting the madness unable to explore and experience the upper dimensions.

You must get to the point where your thoughts, your mind and your love are for the benefit of you and are automatic without forethought. Right now, you are exploring and experiencing your past. It is time to move forward into other dimensions.

Let your marvelous news be that you have shed the programming, you recognize you, you give you "Ultimate Respect" and you explore and experience the Upper Dimensions of The Infinite Spirit.

When you pray
Be sure you meditate to
Step outside of the programming dimensions
Before you pray
Call The Infinite Spirit to
Come and surround you with
Protective energy
Pray to release that programming which
Imprisons you every day
Pray to be enveloped by
The Infinite Spirit
Step out of the programming dimensions
Pray to step into
Dimensions of peace, love, strength, beauty and
Marvelous omnipotence in
The Upper Dimensions of The Infinite Spirit

All Praises to The Infinite Spirit!

I suggest that you listen to the tapes and read the books of Bishop T.D. Jakes and Dr. Bill Winston. Their perspectives relate messages of The Infinite Spirit. Wake up call messages! They know how to awaken your Spirit. They are Spirits of The Infinite Spirit who know their purpose. They are oh so connected to The Infinite Spirit! I love you Bishop Jakes and Dr. Winston! I appreciate your messages from The Infinite Spirit! Thank you!

If you do not already, you must watch the marvelous Oprah Winfrey! She has uplifted so many Spirits! Oprah, Dr. Robin Smith and Dr. Oz ... what a team they are to awaken you to your Spirit physically, mentally and spiritually! I love you Oprah, Dr. Smith and Dr. Oz! Thank you!

Another excellent book to read is "The Science of Success" by James Arthur Ray. He gave me another perspective of "when you think, you create what you think". Mr. Ray said, "What you think about, you bring about". This is another twist giving additional clarification. I love you Mr. Ray! Thank you!

Let's not forget the new craze "The Secret" by Rhonda Byrne. I caution you to know the consequences of asking for and receiving the material things you want ... there are responsibilities. Do not lets your wants ... your wishes put you back into deep debt. Everything has a consequence and or a sacrifice that you will have to make. When you are immersed in the programming, you will not follow the rules of giving you "Ultimate Respect".

Have you seen the series 'The Stand' by Stephen King? His perspective recites more dimension madness and the way to release those maddening dimensions. He depicts those maddening programming dimensions excellently!

Do you see how different perspectives will help you recognize what's really going on? I am not promoting sales. <u>You must listen</u> to all perspectives! We need those twists! The more perspectives you are aware of, the closer you come to exploring and experiencing all the Dimensions of The Infinite Spirit! Someone you listen to may give you the words which will effect a sinking in of "What's Really Going On"! I mean, the programming is invading your blood so deep that a Spirit may never awaken from the Rip Van Winkle sleep that the effects of the programming initiate.

Wake up! Wake up! Wake up!

Message from The Infinite Spirit

"Now it is time for you to come out of My dimensions of programming madness. You have learned the lessons well. It is time to explore and experience My Marvelous Upper Dimensions.

I will tell you what hell and heaven are. Hell is My Lower Dimensions ... My Dimensions of programming for Spirit awakening. Heaven is My Upper Dimensions ... My Dimensions of "Ultimate Respect"

Where are you My Child"?

Spirits of The Infinite Spirit
I enjoyed writing and talking to you
Your "Ultimate Respect" for your Spirit
Will take you to wonderful dimensions of
The Infinite Spirit
I love you!

May your "Ultimate Respect" flourish!

The Infinite Spirit has created and continually creates all and everything.
The Infinite Spirit is magnanimous!

Magnanimous
Great of mind
Elevated above what is low, mean or ungenerous
Dictated by or exhibiting nobleness of soul
Honorable
A loftiness of Spirit
To disdain meanness and revenge
To make sacrifices for worthy ends

The Infinite Spirit gives to your Spirit magnanimous acts
Enabling one to bear trouble calmly

EVERYTHING is of The Infinite Spirit!

All Praises To The Infinite Spirit!

Wake Up Call! It's A Wake Up Call Y'all!

ACKNOWLEDGEMENTS

These are Spirits of The Infinite Spirit whose perspective had or has an impact on my Spirit. Thank you for your lessons and awakenings! I appreciate you all!

The Infinite Spirit ... no doubt!

Ralph Abbott, Jr.   Maya Angelou

Those beautiful folks at Annabelle Lane in Las Vegas ... Ellen, Sue, Terry, Peggy, Eddie, Victoria, Melissa, Karen, Carellyn, Jan, Glenn, Marilyn, and what's his name, the head of maintenance ... he helped me so much when I had to move ... oh yeah! Harry! Love you all!

Thomas Aquinas	Aristotle
Alex Baldwin	Tyra Banks
H.B. Barnum	Terry Barros
Dr. Michael Beckwith	Madame Blavatsky
Betty Brewer	Charles Brewer
Donald Brewer	Donna Brewer
Douglas Brewer	Garry Brewer
Geraldine Smith Brewer	Greg Brewer
Jarid Brewer	Jeffrey Brewer
Rhonda Brewer	Richard Brewer
Sabrina Brewer	Leonard Brown
Buddha	Thomas H. Burgoyne
Rev. Johnny Burns	Coron Burrell
Kenny Burrell	W.E. Butler
Joseph Campbell	George Washington Carver
Bill Cosby	Angela Davis
Babes Delgado	Rosa Delgado
Creflo Dollar	Frederick Douglas
W.E.B. Dubois	Dr. Floyd Flake
Ramona Fraiter	Gandhi
Nikki Giovanni	Chris Gregory
Chuck Gross	Stephen W. Hawking
Gil Scot Heron	Linda Henderson
Anthony Henry	Michelle Henry
Dorothy Brewer Hicks	Jennifer Hicks
Napoleon Hill	Deserie Ann Howe
Emily P. Howe	Shaun Howe
Little Ma Howe – Cheryl	Michelle Howe

Sandy Howe
Darnell Isaacs
Jesse Jackson
Jesus of Nazareth
Jimmy Johnson
Bishop Noel Jones
Kahil Kibran
Enid Malave

The Koran
Malcolm X
Piesy McClure
Tootie McClure

Steveland Morris
Bill Moyers
Neitche
Barack Obama
Joel Osteen
Rev. Russell Patrick
Della Perry
Justine Perry
Frederick K. Price
Dr. Richard M. Restak
Ruth Rivers

Lester Hubble
Ike Isaacs
Bishop T.D. Jakes
Magic Ervin Johnson
Beverly Jones
Florence Jones
Henriette Anne Klauser
Dr. Martin Luther
    King, Jr.
Richard Lett
Marjorie McClure
Tata McClure
The Honorable Elijah
    Mohammed
Monk Montgomery
Mary Murphy
No Eyes
Oprah
Dorothy Parker
Shirley Patrick
Diane Perry
Sandra Perry
James Arthur Ray
Benny Rivers
Don Miguel Ruiz

Sandra _____ who lived in Casa Rosa in Las Vegas in the late 1970's/early 1980's. Sorry my friend! I forgot your last name but, you know I love ya!

Rafaela Santiago   Dr. Robin Smith

Dr. Spiegel, Patty, Dr. Lee & Lisa at Hartford Hospital

Erica & Todnik Stradford

Tammy _____ who now lives in San Diego. I don't think I ever knew her last name ... she was just my daughter Tammy ... a wonderful person! You should meet her? Love ya Tammy!

Booker T. Washington   Dr. Cornell West
Nancy Wilson   Iyanla Van Zant

And, everyone else I came in contact with ... I love you!

BIO
RUTH ISAACS

I have done extensive study in the fields of Psychology, Philosophy and Theosophy. I have worked with children and adults to help them uplift their Spirits with wonderful success. I started writing this book in 1983. Upon completion of the first draft, I was struggling with my attitude, my hurt, my anger and my depression. I was not confident enough to get my book published even though I was uplifting other Spirits. No one was talking about what I was seeing until the 1990's wherein psychologists and the like were talking and writing about what I had written and was talking about ten years earlier ... instant confidence booster!

In 2003, my life changed ... my physical body broke down. I recognized the importance of living my life to the maximum. It finally clicked that I was a Child of The Infinite Creator and, therefore, had to give my Spirit "Ultimate Respect"! I was listening to and trusting what The Infinite Creator was revealing to me. I put trust in the wonderful gifts The Infinite Creator has given me. Oh, yes! I feel very Blessed to be one of The Infinite Creator's Children! All Praises to The Infinite Creator!

I have updated my perspectives from 1983. I have explored and experienced dimensions that are not talked about. Truth must be awakened to and continuously recognized.

SYNOPSIS

When in your quest for purpose and recognition of "What's Really Going On", Wake Up Call One will give insight into things that are important to keep in your Spirit thoughts. You are a Child ... a Spirit of The Infinite Creator who has access to all dimensions of The Infinite Creator of All That Is. Most likely, you are exploring and experiencing the programming in the Lower dimensions of The Infinite Creator. You will cruise in the Upper Dimensions of The Infinite Creator when you recognize what's really going on and awaken to "Ultimate Respect"!

All human Spirits learn the same lessons in different degrees and situations. In the Lower Dimensions of The Infinite Creator, it is taught that these lessons have to be experienced repeatedly until the lesson has been absolutely learned, in a world where there are no absolutes. As you open yourself to the Upper Dimensions of The Infinite Creator, you will see the fallacy of these repeat lessons.

Wake Up Call One will make you think ... think before you do anything ... think before you say anything ... think about what you are going to say ... think about what you are going to do ... think about those consequences getting ready to affect you.

You are a Child ... a Spirit of The Infinite Creator and, therefore, have access to all Dimensions of The Infinite Creator of All That Is. You are a Spirit who will eventually only ride in, on, over, under and around all The Infinite Creator's Magnificent Upper Dimensions. You will not get to cruise unless you recognize "What's Really Going On" ... until you wake up to "Ultimate Respect".

All Praises To The Infinite Creator!

Ruth Isaacs

PUBLISHING YOUR WORK WITH AUTHORHOUSE

Choosing the right publisher among the many companies available is a very critical step towards getting your voice in print. Throughout our exclusive AuthorCentric publishing process, you collaborate with a team of author advocates who will ensure that your vision is translated into a high-quality printed product. We guide you through every step of the book publishing process, from cover design and page layout to distribution and marketing. When you publish your book with AuthorHouse, you can expect to receive expert advice and support while still maintaining intellectual rights to your work and creative control of your book.

Publishing with AuthorHouse

- Publish your work in paperback or hardcover format in a variety of industry standard sizes

- Complete book set-up includes: full-color cover, interior formatting, perfect binding and an in-depth call with your design team to discuss layout, cover and formatting

- Author-set royalty schedule and retail selling prices

- Assignment of ISBN numbers provide worldwide distribution

- Full-color book publishing available

For more information, please visit www.authorhouse.com to request a free Publishing Guide, or call 888.519.5121 to speak with an Author Advocate.

Printed in the United States
88869LV00003B/185/A

9 781425 941185